D1487425

Maine Coast and Islands

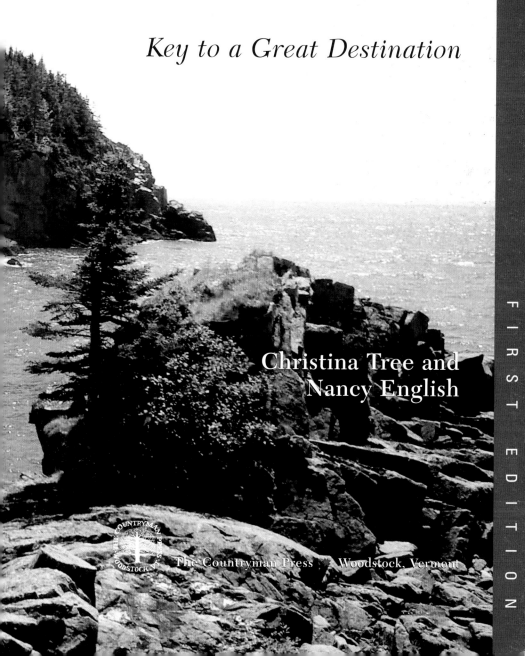

Maine Coast and Islands

Key to a Great Destination

Christina Tree and
Nancy English

The Countryman Press • Woodstock, Vermont

FIRST EDITION

Copyright © 2011 by Christina Tree and Nancy English

All rights reserved. No part of this book may be reproduced in any form or by any electronic or mechanical means including information storage and retrieval systems without permission in writing from the publisher, except by a reviewer, who may quote brief passages.

Maine Coast and Islands: Key to a Great Destination
ISBN 978-1-58157-137-0

Front cover photograph by Carol Latta, a photographer and painter whose work focuses on the lighthouses, ships, and natural beauty of the Maine coastline. To see and purchase her work, visit www.amazingmaine.com.

Interior photographs by the authors unless otherwise specified
Maps by Erin Greb Cartographhpy, © The Countryman Press
Book design by Bodenweber Design
Composition by PerfecType, Nashville, TN

Published by The Countryman Press, P.O. Box 748, Woodstock, VT 05091
Distributed by W. W. Norton & Company, Inc., 500 Fifth Avenue, New York, NY 10110
Printed in the United States of America

10 9 8 7 6 5 4 3 2 1

For Bill Davis,
companion on many thousands
of Maine miles

CT

To the residents of Maine,
who take good care of
the most beautiful place I know.

NE

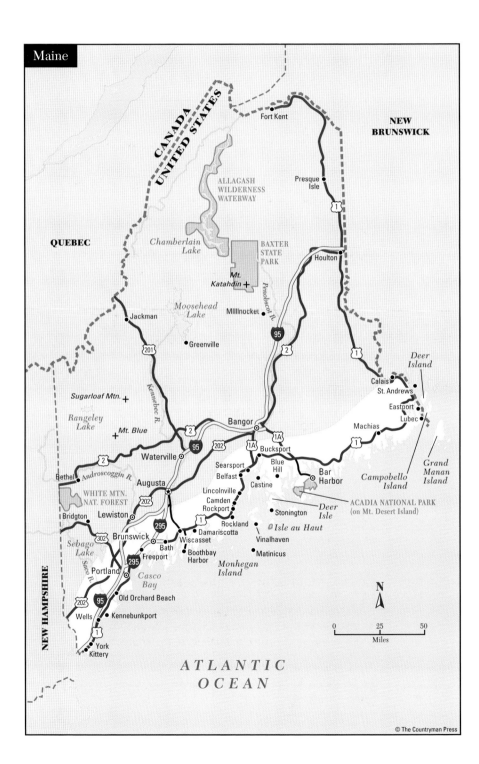

Contents

Maps

Basics

LAY OF THE LAND:
WATER, WATER EVERYWHERE

The Maine coast is lengthier, more varied, and more accessible than most visitors assume. Kittery on Maine's southern border is officially just 211 driving miles southeast of Bar Harbor and 293 from Eastport, but the shoreline between Kittery and Eastport measures more than 4,500 miles—and some 7,000 miles if you count offshore islands.

That's more than the rest of the East Coast combined.

In contrast with much of this country's East Coast and most of the West Coast, Maine's shoreline rarely faces open ocean. With the exception of a sandy arc of land along the South Coast and a high, rocky stretch of Way Down East headlands known as the Bold Coast—both measuring less than 40 miles—the shore corkscrews in and out of coves and points, winding along bays and up wide, tidal rivers. More than a dozen ragged peninsulas extend like so many fingers south from Rt. 1, separating the bays and rivers, notched in turn with numerous coves and harbors.

In many places islands are "hinged" to the mainland by bridges and causeways. Scientists tell us that the peninsulas and offshore islands are mountains drowned by the same glaciers that sculpted the area's many shallow, (relatively) warm-water lakes. The tides shift from high to low roughly every 12 hours; these shifts are more extreme as you move northeast, measuring a difference of 9 feet in Kittery, 25 at Eastport.

Current offshore vessels tend to be leisure craft, fishing boats, and lobster boats, but for more than two centuries these waters were busy freight and passenger lanes. It's because visitors arrived primarily by water prior to the 1920s that summer resorts—from Popham Beach and Boothbay Harbor to Bar Harbor—are at the tips of peninsulas and hinged islands, miles from Rt. 1.

The Good News: This lengthy and convoluted shoreline harbors a wide choice of places to sleep as well as to walk and to eat within sound and sight of water. Access to coastal preserves has been dramatically increased in recent decades by both state and conservation groups.

Sleep within earshot of the water at Coveside Bed & Breakfast, Five Islands.   Christina Tree

The waters that splinter the coast ensure the distinctive character of the many, relatively isolated communities. The feel as well as the shape of the coast changes as you travel northeast. The lightly settled and touristed region beyond the turnoff for Bar Harbor is a very different Maine from the heavily populated and touristed South Coast. Still, the moment you cross the southern border, you know you're in Maine. Kittery and York both have their share of coves and rocky paths, and local accents are as strong as any to be found in Eastport.

The Bad News: You can't rush. The chief complaint among Maine visitors is "not enough time." The shape of the coast and two-lane nature of Rt. 1, the coastal highway, hobbles attempts to try to reach Acadia National Park from points south on a summer weekend, especially a long weekend.

The Key: Most visitors come to Maine for R&R. So turn off Rt. 1. Savor the salt air and the scenery in a lobster-boat-filled harbor. Slow down. Walk a shore path. Eat lobster in a real lobster pound. Talk to a local. Get out on the water ASAP.

Rock Gardens Inn on the Phippsburg Peninsula   Christina Tree

Maine Speak

Down East is a nautical term referring to the way the way the wind generally blows along the Maine coast: out of the southwest, ushering sailing vessels down-wind and east. Moreover, the coast itself generally runs east more than north. This phenomenon is painfully obvious if you happen to be driving "south" on Rt. 1 at sunset. To further confuse the issue, coastal highways are labeled "north" and "south." Also: *Down* usually refers to traveling east. So instead of driving up north from Kittery to Bar Harbor, you are heading "Down East." In *Sense of Place* you discover that from the beginning of settlement the coast was divided into eastern and western Maine at the Kennebec River. However, "Down East" as a place is now equated only with the parts of Maine from Blue Hill Peninsula on "down."

REGIONS AT A GLANCE

South Coast

This 36-mile-stretch of coast accounts for 90 percent of Maine beaches. Many visitors get no farther. Family-geared lodging, from vintage motor courts to condo-style complexes, predominates. Dining options include some of the state's foremost restaurants as well as plenty of places to eat lobster, ice cream, and saltwater taffy. You'll find summer theater and a fine art museum in Ogunquit (ogunquit.org); a glimpse of colonial times in The Museums of Old York (oldyork.org); and a sense of the shipbuilding era in the fine old sea captains' houses in Kennebunkport (visitthekennebunks.com), as well as a fine Seashore Trolley Museum (trolley museum.org). There are brand-name outlets in Kittery (thekitteryoutlets.com); boardwalks in York Beach (gatewaytomaine.org) and Old Orchard Beach (old orchardbeachmaine.com). Everywhere is the promise of endless sand. Luckily the lay of the land—salt marsh, estuarine reserves, and other wetlands—limits commercial clutter.

The Pier at Old Orchard Beach   Nancy English

Portland and Casco Bay

Lively, walkable, sophisticated, Maine's largest city is also a working port facing an island-studded bay. Visitors head for the Portland Museum of Art (portlandmuseum.org) and then down Congress St. to the Old Port (visitport land.com), more than five square blocks built exuberantly during the city's peak shipping era and now laced with restaurants, cafés, shops, and galleries. From the waterfront Casco Bay Line (cascobaylines.com) ferries ply the bay, stopping at islands. Beyond the Old Port the two sights not to miss

Weatherbeaten by Winslow Homer, circa 1916   Courtesy of Portland Museum of Art, bequest of Charles Shipman Payson

are Portland Head Light (portlandheadlight.com) in Fort Williams Park on Cape Elizabeth, and Portland Observatory (portlandlandmarks.org) on Munjoy Hill. Less than 20 miles north of Portland, Freeport (freeportusa.com) is Maine's premier shopping destination, anchored by L.L. Bean (llbean.com), open 24 hours, surrounded by 74 more upscale outlets.

At the Portland Farmers' Markets   Nancy English

Midcoast

The 100 miles of Rt. 1 between Brunswick and Bucksport are generally equated with Maine's Midcoast—but this region's depth is far greater. It extends south from Rt. 1 to the tips of roughly a dozen peninsulas and attached islands, 10 miles at Boothbay Harbor (boothbayharbor.com), a dozen to Pemaquid Point's famed lighthouse (lighthousefoundation.org), as well as inland to river and lake towns. Inviting old communities, all with lodging, dining, and shopping, anchor Rt. 1. Brunswick (brunswickdowntown.org) offers summer theater, music, and the Bowdoin College (bowdoin.edu) museums. In Bath (visitbath.com) the Maine Maritime Museum (mainemaritimemuseum.org) is a must-see. Wiscasset (midcoastmaine.com) is known for antiques and Damariscotta (damariscottaregion.com), for oysters. Rockland (therealmaine.com)—home to the Farnsworth Museum and Wyeth Center (farnsworthmuseum.org)—is also the departure point for most Windjammers (sailmainecoast.com) and Maine State Ferries (exploremaine.com). With its sea captains' houses and antiques shops Camden (visitcamden.com) is a justly famous resort, while Belfast (belfastmaine.org) and Searsport, home to the Penobscot Marine Museum (penobscotmarinemuseum.org), both evoke Maine's seafaring era.

The Lobster Shack at Two Lights, Cape Elizabeth

Nancy English

Boothbay Harbor

Christina Tree

The dramatic new Penobscot Narrows Bridge (maine.gov/observatory) visually underscores the sense of turning a major coastal corner. From its observatory, 43 stories above the Penobscot River, you look off down Penobscot Bay and across the green shoreline curving eastward. What you see is is the **Blue Hill Peninsula** (bluehill peninsula.org) and a land finger with **Castine** (castine.me.us) at its tip. Deer Isle and **Stonington** (deerisle.com) straggle south from Blue Hill, off beyond the horizon. Here the intermingling of land and water creates a landscape that's exceptional, even in Maine. It's seasonal home to the state's largest concentration of artists and craftspeople, writers and musicians.

Rockland Harbor Trail   Christina Tree

While the major villages all offer fine galleries, studios are also salted along scenic roads, which lead to numerous preserves with water views.

Stonington Harbor   Christina Tree

Acadia

Mount Desert (pronounced *dessert*) is New England's second largest island, one conveniently linked to the mainland south of Ellsworth (ellsworth chamber.org) by a causeway and bridge. Two-fifths of its 108 square miles are maintained as Acadia National Park (nps.gov/acad), laced with roads geared to touring by car; you'll also find more than 50 miles of "carriage roads" reserved for biking and skiing and 120 miles of hiking trails. The beauty of "MDI" cannot be overstated. Twenty-six mountains rise abruptly from the sea and from the

"The Bubbles" at Jordan Pond

Nancy English

shores of four lakes. Mount Cadillac, at 1,532 feet, is the highest point on the U.S. Atlantic seaboard. Its broad summit, accessible by car, is said to offer the first view of sunrise in the United States, but it attracts a larger crowd at sunset. The island seems larger than it is because it's almost bisected by Somes Sound, a natural fjord dividing it almost in two. On one side is the lively resort village of Bar Harbor (barharbormaine.com), gateway to Acadia; on the other are the more laid-back yachting villages of Northeast (mountdesertchamber.org) and Southwest Harbors (acadiachamber.com), along with the more workaday fishing village of Bass Harbor.

Down East

At the junction of Rts. 3 and 1 in Ellsworth, it's Rt. 3 that shoots straight ahead toward Bar Harbor and Rt. 1 that angles off, the road less taken. The 27 miles along Rt. 1 that begin at the Hancock/Sullivan Bridge and loop around Schoodic Peninsula (acadia-schoodic.org) to Winter Harbor are a National Scenic Byway, while the drive around Schoodic Point is a part of Acadia National Park. Sadly, few tourists continue on down Rt. 1 into Washington County, a bleakly beautiful landscape of thick pine forests, blueberry barrens, and 700 miles of coast with dramatic cliffs and deep tidal bays carved by the highest tides on the eastern seaboard. Pickups outnumber cars, and lobster boats way outnumber pleasure craft. History is glimpsed in the graceful 1818 Ruggles House

Head of Harbour Light, Campobello

Christina Tree

View from Lubec

Christina Tree

(ruggleshouse.org) in Columbia Falls, the 1770s Burnham Tavern (burnham tavern.com) in Machias (machiaschamber.org), and Roosevelt Campobello International Park (fdr.net), accessed from Lubec (westquoddy.com). Birders head out from Jonesport (jonesport.com) or Cutler (boldcoast.com) to Machias Seal Island for a close-up view of puffins. Eastport (eastportchamber.net), 82 miles northeast of Bar Harbor, draws artists with its northern light, fine architecture, and end-of-the-world feel.

Monhegan

Liam Davis

Islands

There are 4,617 coastal Maine islands, but just 14 now support year-round communities, compared with 300 in the 19th century. Overnight lodging can be found on Chebeague Island (chebeague.org) and Long Island (chestnuthillinn.com) in Casco Bay, accessible from Portland. The major island destinations are Monhegan, Vinalhaven, North Haven, Isle au Haut, Swan's Island, and Campobello. Each is different but all share a community closeness and a way of welcoming visitors on their own terms. Monhegan (monhegan.com), 11 miles out to sea, is barely a square mile, with less than 70 year-round residents. It attracts the largest number of day-trippers, thanks to excursion boats from Boothbay Harbor and New Harbor as well as ferries from Port Clyde. It also offers the widest choice of island lodging, including two vintage summer hotels. It has attracted prominent artists since the 1850s. Most of the island has been preserved as common space, laced by 17 miles of walking trails.

The islands with overnight lodging that are most easily accessed by frequent Maine State Ferry (exploremaine.org) service are Vinalhaven (vinalhaven.org) and North Haven (nebolodge.com). Both are roughly a dozen miles from Rockland but separated from each other by a narrow passage. Vinalhaven is Maine's largest offshore island and supports its largest year-round community and lobster fleet. Here visitors find food, lodging in Carver's Harbor, a 0.25-mile walk from the ferry. Half the size, North Haven is summer home to some of the country's wealthiest families; the few shops and restaurants are within steps of the dock. On Mount Desert you can day-trip from Bass Harbor to Swan's Island (swansisland.com) and Frenchboro (bassharborcruises.com). Easily accessible from Northeast Harbor and Southwest Harbor, Little Cranberry Island (islesford.com) offers good food, a museum, and galleries as well as views.

North Haven   Christina Tree

If You Have Just a Weekend

Pick a South Coast resort. Visit Portland.

If You Have a Week

The average initial visit to Maine is five days, just long enough to decide where you might want to spend more time on your next trip. More than 80 percent of first-time visitors return.

Maine's most popular resort towns—Ogunquit, Old Orchard Beach, Kennebunkport, Boothbay Harbor, and Camden—offer the coast's lion's share of lodging and are spaced like a giant's stepping-stones on the way to Bar Harbor. Spend a night or two on the South Coast, a day in Portland, and then a couple of nights along the Midcoast on your way to Acadia National Park. If you want to get off the beaten track (Rt. 1), pick a peninsula or two to explore on the way to or from Mount Desert. If you really want a sense of Maine, spend a night or two (don't just day-trip) on Monhegan or Vinalhaven, and/or continue beyond Mount Desert to Lubec and Eastport.

But everyone is different. For six suggested itineraries, see the end of this chapter.

Timing

High season along the Maine coast is short: July 4–Labor Day.

Lodging is easier and sometimes cheaper midweek, even in August. If you do want an August weekend at a modest price, reserve far ahead. June can be glorious but weather is chancier, and many visitors book at the last minute. September days are golden and generally clear; most seasonal businesses stay open through Columbus Day.

Portland attracts visitors year-round; in November they tend to stop en route at outlets in Kittery and push on to those in Freeport. January through April is off-season—and with reason—although there's a certain romance to a cozy inns by the sea, especially popular around Valentine's Day. In May alewives return to Damariscotta and beach-walkers, to the South Coast.

Weather and What to Bring

Weather is something you notice more in Maine than most places because it's literally in your face. The sun can be shining brightly along Rt. 1 while a nearby beach, peninsula point, or island is shrouded in fog. Even in August temperatures can begin down along the frost line and soar by midday, only to plunge again at night. It's the Labrador Current from Canada that cools the ocean here, chilling the water to below comfort level for most of us but also bringing that refreshing breeze. Tote a light backpack to shed or add clothing. Maine is all about comfort. Wear a visor or baseball cap, even if you never do ordinarily. Don't be shy about wearing a wool cap and gloves out on the water. Windbreakers, lightweight pants, and comfortable shoes are acceptable dress in most restaurants. Don't forget to pack your camera and binoculars.

If you plan to visit to visit Roosevelt Campobello International Park (fdr.net) on Campobello Island, you also need a passport or passport card (see getyouhome.gov).

Morning fog at Rock Gardens Inn, Sebasco

Christina Tree

TRANSPORTATION

Getting There

By Air

Portland International Jetport (201-774-7301; portlandjetport.org) is connected by major carriers to destinations throughout the country and Canada. Just off I-95, it offers all the major rental cars, also taxi and bus service into Portland.

US Customs, Lubec   Christina Tree

Bangor International Airport (207-947-0384; flybangor.com) is the closest major airport to Bar Harbor with connections to East Coast destinations. Bar Harbor Airport (bhbairport.com)offers connections via Colgan Air to Logan. Knox County Regional Airport (knoxcounty.midcoast.com /departments/airports) is in Rockland.

Logan International Airport in Boston (loganinternationalairport.com) offers the widest choice of both domestic and international flights, and Manchester/Boston Regional Airport (flymanchester.com) is also worth checking; both are linked by

Mermaid Transport (gomermaid.com) and Concord Coach Lines (concord-coachlines.com) with Portland.

By Train

Amtrak's Downeaster (thedowneaster .com) offers five daily roundtrips between Boston's North Station and Portland's rail-bus station just off I-95. It's 2½ hours each way and the way a train ride should be: comfortable and scenic. The first Maine stop is in Wells; then Saco, just beyond the mighty falls; and Old Orchard Beach, within walking distance of the sand and amusement park.

Amtrak's Downeaster links Portland with Boston.

By Bus

Concord Coach Lines (800-639-3317; concordcoachlines.com) serves Portland (where its terminal adjoins Amtrak's), Brunswick, Bath, Wiscasset, Damariscotta, Waldoboro, Rockland, Camden, Belfast, and Searsport. It also offers a popular express from Boston's Logan Airport and South Station to Portland (where the terminal also serves Amtrak), and on to Bangor. Greyhound Bus Lines (800-231-2222; greyhound.com) also links Boston with Portland (where the terminal is old and grungy), Brunswick, and Bangor. The seasonal Bar Harbor Shuttle (207-479-5911; barharborshuttle.com) links both Concord Coach and Greyhound terminals in Bangor with Bar Harbor. West's Coastal Connection (800-565-2823; west busservice.com) offers a similar service to Machias and Perry (the Rt.1 turnoff for Eastport) with flag-down stops in between.

By Car

Most Maine visitors come by car or pick up a rental as soon as they arrive. Check airport websites for rental options.

GETTING AROUND

Highways

The first thing you notice about I-95 in Maine is the way exits are numbered. Each represents mileage from the southern border at Kittery. I-95 becomes the Maine Turnpike (maineturnpike.com) in Kittery, site of a welcome center maintained by the Maine Tourism Association (mainetourism.com). It's stocked with handouts on everything to see and do in the state, operated by knowledgeable staffers, and offers restrooms, maps, pine-shaded picnic tables, and vending machines. Toll-booths begin in York (Exit 7). The first and only service area for coastal travelers is at Kennebunk. The turnpike extends 100 miles, turning inland beyond Portland. Exit 44 puts you on I-295, which takes you another 17 highway miles. Just the first 76 miles of Maine's coastal routes are multilane highway. At I-295, Exit 28, you hit Rt. 1, the mostly two-lane highway for the remaining 217 miles to Eastport. After several initial stoplights there are few traffic signals along its length.

For Traffic Updates
Check the Maine DOT website: 511.maine.gov. Or call 511 or 866-282-7578.

Maps
The state map is free but not great. The AAA map for Northern New England is a step up. Sooner or later Maine explorers pick up *The Maine Atlas and Gazetteer* (DeLorme), available throughout the state.

Are We There Yet?
Boston to Portland: 108 miles, average 2 hours.
   Portland to Bar Harbor: 175 miles, theoretically 3½ hours but good luck!

Shortcuts
I-295, Exit 28 for Brunswick, puts you on Coastal Rt. 1. During peak travel times, you might want to avoid the backup in Brunswick and take I-295, Exit 32, instead. Follow signs for Rt. 1 and stick to middle lanes on Rt. 196.
   Around Rockland: Take Rt. 90 off Rt. 1 in West Warren to Rockport, just south of Camden.
   To Belfast East and Blue Hill/Deer Isle: I-295 to Augusta to I-95 to Exit 113 (Rt. 3) to Belfast, then Rt. 1 east to Rt. 15.
   Quickest way to Bar Harbor: Either the above route or Exit I-95 in Bangor to I-395 to Rt. 1A.

Car-Free
Check out the Maine Department of Transportation's website (exploremaine.org) for airport sites; train, private, and state ferry schedules; and local bus shuttles. *Suggestions:* Take Amtrak's Downeaster (thedowneaster.com) to Wells and use Shoreline Explorer (shorelineexplorer.com) trolleys and buses to access lodging and beaches. The Downeaster also sets you within walking distance of lodging and beach in Old Orchard and at a station with frequent shuttle service to downtown Portland, from which Casco Bay Line Ferries tour the bay. Concord Trailways drops you in Rockland at the ferry terminal; from there you'll find frequent service to Vinalhaven and North Haven (both navigable by bike). Fly or bus to Bar Harbor and use the peerless, free Acadia Shuttle (explore acadia.com) to get around.

Trains
Maine Eastern Railroad (866-637-2457; maineeasternrailroad.com) is a seasonal, shoreline excursion train running 54 miles between Brunswick and Rockland, stopping regularly in Bath and Wiscasset. From Ellsworth,

The Maine Eastern RR   Christina Tree

East Coast Ferry from Eastport to Deer Island, NB

Christina Tree

Downeast Scenic Rail (207-667-7819; downeastscenicrail.org) offers a tranquil excursion inland.

Ferries

Check exploremaine.org for state ferries (see *Islands*, above). The site also offers an overview of both public and private ferries. The major private companies include Casco Bay Lines (casco baylines.com), based in Portland; Monhegan Boat Line (monhegan-boat.com) in Port Clyde; Isle au Haut Ferry Service (isleauhaut.com) in Stonington; and seasonal East Coast Ferries (eastcoastferries.nb.ca) linking Eastport with New Brunswick.

By Schooner

Rockland and Camden (both served by bus) are departure points for Maine Windjammer cruises (sailmaine coast.com) throughout Penoscot Bay. The world's largest fleet of passenger-carrying coastal schooners, these Windjammers are a dozen graceful tall ships, most individually owned. Many

Maine State Ferry at Vinalhaven

Christina Tree

Information Sources

The **Maine Office of Tourism** maintains visitmaine.com and a 24-hour information line (888-624-6345) that connects with a live call center. Request the thick, help-ful, four-season guide *Maine Invites You* (accompanied by a Maine highway map). The guide is published by the **Maine Tourism Association** (207-623-0363; maine tourism.com). The MTA also maintains well-stocked and -staffed welcome centers with restrooms, most with WiFi. Its southern gateway center at **Kittery** (207-439-1319) on I-95 northbound (also accessible from Rt. 1) is a must place to stop. Oth-ers are found in **Yarmouth** on Rt. 1 just off-295, Exit 17 (207-846-0833); in **West Gardiner** at the I-95 service plaza, also accessible from I-295 (207-582-0160); in **Hampden** near Bangor on I-95 both northbound and southbound (207-862-6628); and in **Calais** (207-454-1319) at 39 Union St., geared to southbound visitors. Online or at the information center you can request copies of *The Maine Birding Trail*, *Maine Art Museum Trail*, *The Maine Golf Trail*, and *The Guide to Inns and Bed & Breakfasts and Camps and Cottages*.

are 19th-century vessels, some restored by their present captains. Most carry less than 30 passengers. All offer four- to six-day sails in Penobscot Bay, usually stop-ping to go ashore in small villages and on islands. The schedule is determined by wind and current.

The last fishing schooner built in New England, the *American Eagle* is now a great way to sail.
Fred LeBlanc, courtesy of Maine Windjammer Asssociation

Suggested Itinerary

FOR ART LOVERS

Artists lured Maine's early tourists, and both traditional landscape and contemporary art here continue to be outstanding. Portland and Rockland are home to the coast's two major art museums; both communities support numerous galleries and host Art Walks on the first Friday of each month. Check out the Maine Art Museum Trail (maineartmuseum.org).

Portland First Friday Art Walks (firstfridayartwalk.com) fill the sidewalks of Congress St. with gallerygoers, and the Portland Museum of Art (portlandmuseum.org) is free. The event is the brainchild of Andres Verzosa of Aucocisco Galleries (aucocisco .com), always a worthwhile stop. Maine College of Art's own gallery, The Institute of Contemporary Art at the Maine College of Art (meca.edu),

presents contemporary exhibits, with lectures and workshops. Salt Institute for Documentary Studies (salt.edu) depicts aspects of Maine life. Space Gallery (space538.org) presents unconventional art. Many more venues exhibit artwork, from coffee shops to shops with artisan and craftswork for sale.

Rockland Art Walks are supported by the 21-gallery Arts in Rockland (AIR) association (artsinrockland.com) and the Farnsworth Art Museum and Wyeth Center (farnsworthmuseum .org), which offers free admission every Wednesday evening as well as on first Fridays. The Farnsworth's permanent collection exhibits Maine's iconic artists from the 19th through 20th centuries and contemporary artists; changing exhibits vary. Rockland's leading galleries include Caldbeck Gallery (cald beck.com); Harbor Square Gallery (harborsquaregallery.com), filling three floors of a 1912 building at 374 Main St.; the Eric Hopkins Gallery (eric hopkins.com), showcasing work by one

Monhegan Houses by Edward Hopper, circa 1916   Courtesy of Portland Museum of Art, Bernstein Acquisition Fund

Farnsworth Art Museum, Rockland
Courtesy, Farnsworth Art Museum

of Maine's most popular and distinctive artists; and **Archipelago Fine Arts** (thearchipelago.net) at the Island Institute, representing some 300 artists and craftspeople on Maine Islands.

Smaller and seasonal but significant gallery clusters are found in the villages of **Blue Hill, Deer Isle,** and **Stonington,** all spaced along Rt. 15 as it winds down the peninsula and linked islands that define eastern rim of Penobscot Bay. Standouts include the **Leighton** (leightongallery.com) and **Jud Hartmann Gallery** (judhartmann gallery.com) galleries in Blue Hill, and the **Turtle** (turtlegallery.com) and **Lester** (thelestergalleryllc.com)

View of Penobscot Bay from Caterpillar Hill, Sedgwick, by Jill Hoy

galleries in Deer Isle. In Stonington— which also observes first Fridays with receptions at some dozen galleries July–Oct.—look for the **Jill Hoy** (jill hoy.com), **gWatson** (gwatsongallery .com), and **Isalos Fine Art** (isalosfine art.com) galleries.

The island of **Monhegan,** the subject of many of Maine's most famous paintings, continues to draw summer artists from throughout the country. Their work is showcased in the **Lupine Gallery** near the ferry landing. Pick up a map/guide to the studios of roughly 20 resident artists who welcome visitors.

Suggested Itinerary

FOR BEACHCOMBERS

The coastline of southern Maine offers some classic vistas of endless sand, a few beaches that stretch past the horizon, and several curved beaches that embrace ocean waves. **Long Sands Beach** in York Beach is a 2-mile arc of gray sand with good-sized ocean waves, bordered by sand that's wide at low tide and narrow at high, backed by parking spots along a street lined with summer rentals. Restaurants, shops, and old-style amusements cluster at the far end of the beach. Another stretch that draws a crowd is **Old Orchard Beach,** with its centerpiece Pier and its famous french fries, bars, and restaurants. The Amtrak Downeaster from Boston to Portland stops right in the middle of the beach.

Gooch's Beach in Kennebunk offers a view of Kennebunk River traffic at one end, and is a favorite spot for surfers. Buy a beach parking permit at

A day at the beach at Reid State Park

Christina Tree

the town offices or the police station, or at the chamber of commerce. Goose Rocks Beach, at the northern end of Kennebunkport's coastline (Kennebunk is south of the river, Kennebunkport north) is secluded and peaceful just off Rt. 9, but a parking permit is required from the Kennebunkport Police Station.

If you would just as soon skip Maine's prime beach resorts but still like to walk long beaches and are curious to test the waves, two neighboring Midcoast peninsulas offer inviting options. Check out **Popham Beach State Park** and **Reid State Park** (maine.gov/cgi-bin/online/doc/park search/index.pl) in "Brunswick and the Harpswells."

Suggested Itinerary

FOR BIRDERS

Warblers, chickadees, cardinals, starlings, and crows love the busy South Coast, and the northern thrush, vireo, boreal chickadee, and gray jay can be seen, with luck. Along the ocean the great blue heron can rise from a salt marsh anywhere from Peaks Island off Portland to Machias. Kingfishers dive for fish by Tenants Harbor near Pemaquid Point, bald eagles coast serene as the air itself on the Bagaduce River near Blue Hill, and ospreys bring dinner back to their nest off the docks at Robinhood Marina south of Bath.

Maine's destination birding season begins with a May Wings, Waves and Woods Festival in Deer Isle (deer isle.com), then a Spring Birding Festival (downeastbirdfest.org), celebrated Memorial Day weekend in the Lubec area with self-guided and guided hikes; the Acadia Birding Festival (acadia birdingfestival.com) takes place the following week. June and July are prime months for viewing puffins up close on Machias Seal Island (see *Puffin-Watching*), accessed from nearby Cutler. In September hawks circle lazily above Mount Agamenticus in York, and birders flock to Monhegan Island

This solitary sandpiper was photographed by Karl Gerstenberger Karl Gerstenberger

(kegerstenberger.zenfolio.com)

Puffin-Watching

Maine's colorful Atlantic puffins lay just one egg a year. They were almost extinct at the turn of the 20th century, when the only surviving birds nested on either **Matinicus Rock** or **Machias Seal Island.** Since 1973 Audubon has helped reintroduce nesting on **Eastern Egg Rock** in Muscongus Bay, 6 miles off Pemaquid Point, and since 1984 there has been a similar puffin-restoration project on Seal Island in outer Penobscot Bay. The time to view puffins is June through early August. The only place you are allowed to view the birds up close on land is **Machias Seal Island,** and visitors are strictly limited. We recommend signing on with **Bold Coast Charters** (bold coast.com) in Cutler. Puffins are smaller than generally realized, but with the help of binoculars you can also view the birds from the water on tours with **Hardy Boat Cruises** (hardyboat.com) from New Harbor, and the **Monhegan Boat Line** (monheganboat.com) from Port Clyde. The **Hog Island Audubon Camp** (maineaudubon.org) offers guided boat cruises to Eastern Egg Rock. **Project Puffin Visitor Center** (projectpuffin.org) in Rockland uses live-streaming mini cams and audio to provide a virtual visit with nesting puffins on Machias Seal Island.

Puffins on Machias Seal Island

Christina Tree

to record the fall migration. Through-out the year check with Maine Audubon (maineaudubon.org). It's based at Gisland Farm in Falmouth, with programs in Scarborough Marsh, Merrymeeting Bay, and weeklong summer programs at Hog Island Audubon Camp near New Harbor, which is also departure point for Hardy Boat Cruises circling Egg Rock (again, see *Puffin-Watching*). View or download a superb free *Maine Birding Trail* map/guide to 82 Maine birding sites at mainebirding trail.com; you can also request a glossy print version online or at one of the Maine Tourism Association welcome centers. Also see mainebirding.com for trip planning, and tours and the sidebar on birding in the "Western Penobscot Bay" chapter.

This photo of a lesser yellowlegs is another by Karl Gerstenberger, online at kegersten berger.zenfolio.com

Karl Gerstenberger

At the Portland Farmers' Markets

Nancy English

Suggested Itinerary

FOR FOODIES

Portland offers the highest concentration of renowned dining spots (see that chapter). Dining in Rockland and Camden is also terrific. But on and near Mount Desert Island, there is another subset of excellence. In Southwest Harbor look for Red Sky (red skyrestaurant.com) and Xanthus at The Claremont Hotel (theclaremont hotel.com). Also outstanding: Town Hill Bistro (townhillbistro.com) on Rt. 102 in Bar Harbor and Burning Tree in Otter Creek, with its own organic gardens. All offer well-made meals and a track record in a region of restaurants that are open one summer and gone the next. On Cottage St. in Bar Harbor, Mache Bistro (machebistro .com)—run by well-known chef-owner Kyle Yardborough—offers great dining. Most exciting of all is the fresh, local, and Mediterranean cuisine at Ellsworth's Cleonice (cleonice.com). Count on the season dictating the

Gifts from the Sea

Cod and pollack are still found in Maine waters, along with Atlantic sturgeon, alewife and striped bass, yellowtail flounder, halibut, and haddock. Atlantic salmon are ever rarer, but farmed salmon are plentiful and local. Soft-shell clams remain abundant and oysters, especially in Damarsicotta, are making a comeback. Hard-shell lobsters are, however, what Maine is known for worldwide.

Maine's clean, cold waters produce the planet's tastiest **lobster** (lobsterfrommaine.com). This hard-shelled crustacean has a long body and five sets of legs, including two large front claws, one large, flat, and heavy and the other smaller, thinner. Lobsters don't like light, hiding by day and emerging at night to eat mussels, sea urchins, and crabs. Most are at least seven years old by the time they are caught because Maine regulates the minimum (also maximum) size of what can be sold. The state also prohibits catching pregnant females, and imposes trap limits and license controls.

Salmon farms off Campobello Island
Christina Tree

Lobster feast with all the fixings
Jim Dugan, courtesy of Maine Windjammer Association

In the 1880s most lobster was canned. Currently 90 percent of what's caught by Maine's 7,500 lobstermen is shipped live, out of state. Maine lobster harvests have actually tripled since the early 1990s. Prices also climbed until 2007 but have taken a dramatic dip since then for a variety of reasons. Chief among these, lobstermen will tell you, has been distribution through Canadian processors to large chain restaurants and cruise lines rather than more local and targeted marketing. Even locally, however, lobsterman are frustrated by inflated lobster prices still on the menu at tourist restaurants. The best places to consume this tasty crustacean remain lobster pounds.

menu, and understand that "day-boat" next to the halibut means the fish was landed almost precisely yesterday. The terrific tapas show off chef-owner Rich Hanson's power to persuade the locals, who make this place hop year-round.

Suggested Itinerary

FOR SHOPPERS

Outlet devotees head for **Kittery** (the kitteryoutlets.com) and **Freeport** (freeportusa.com). Both outlet centers repeat many of the name brands, but Freeport adds to the mix the flagship store of **L.L. Bean** (llbean.com), with a campus that includes stores devoted to hunting and fishing; to bike, boat, and ski; and more. There are also free workshops. **L.L. Bean Discovery School** (llbean.com/ods) is the best place of all to try out a new sport or take an hour to get a handle on kayaking. The company also sponsors free summer concerts (llbean.com/events). **Freeport Village Station** (onefreeportvillagestation.com), a complex across from the Bean campus, houses Coach, Nike, Brooks Brothers, and Calvin Klein, also the L.L. Bean Outlet.

Renys in Bath Christina Tree

Kittery claims 120 outlets in a series of shopping centers strung along 1.3 miles of Rt. 1; these are less appealing because less walkable, but for shoppers from points south, they are more than an hour closer than Freeport. The anchor store here is the **Kittery Trading Post** (kitterytradingpost.com). **Stonehill Kitchen** (stonehillkitchen.com) in nearby York, just off I-95, Exit 7, is a major draw for fans of its products and Maine specialty foods, as well as for those who just want to sample them. **Portland's Old Port** is fun, and there's an intriguing stretch of shopping at the foot of **Munjoy Hill**, across from the Eastern Cemetery. Check out **Ferdinand** (ferdinandhomestore.com), with quirky motifs and inexpensive hipster trinkets, and **Angela Adams** (angelaadams.com), with high design, nationally recognized rugs, and women's purses.

The two Midcoast towns of **Bath** (visitbath.com) and **Damariscotta** (damariscottaregion.com) offer a particularly rewarding mix of small shops. Damaricotta is home base for **Renys** (renys.com), a family-owned Maine chain of 14 discount stores that fill the void and, as in Bath, the very spaces left by defunct department stores. Listing what Renys stocks is harder than listing what it doesn't.

Sherman's Book & Stationery Store in Boothbay Harbor

Christina Tree

Maine is famed for the quality of its potters; worth a detour are Georgetown Pottery (georgetownpottery.com) in its tiny namesake village south of Bath, Edgecomb Potters (edgecombpotters.com) on the way down Rt. 27 to the Boothbays, and Columbia Falls Pottery (columbiafallspottery.com) just off Rt. 1 way Down East on your way to Eastport, where Raye's Mustard Mill (rayesmustard.com) is the place to stop.

Suggested Itinerary

FOR LIGHTHOUSE BUFFS

As the state's 68 lighthouses have become automated, many have been adopted by "Friends," volunteers dedicated to restoring them. Each year more lights welcome visitors, some only on special days and others regularly throughout the summer season. Some are easily accessible by land or on regularly accessible islands; others, only by excursion boat. The state's iconic images are of Neddick (Nubble) Light, within camera range just off Sohier Park in York. Portland Head Light (portlandheadlight.com) on Cape Elizabeth is a must-stop. Completed in 1790, automated in 1990, it now offers delightful museum featuring the history of lighthouses. Since its appearance on the Maine quarter, the vintage-1824 Pemaquid Point Lighthouse (lighthousefoundation.org) has become the best known of all. Its tower is now open seasonally; its Keeper's House is The Fisherman's Museum (207-677-2494).

Rockland's Gateway Visitor Center is home to the Maine Lighthouse Museum (mainelighthousemuseum.com), and at 464 Main St. the American

Lighthouse Foundation (lighthouse foundation.org) offers its own interpretive center. South of Rockland the Marshall Point Light (marshallpoint .org) at Port Clyde, a small light built on a scenic point in 1885, is open seasonally, along with a museum in the former keeper's home. The American Lighthouse Foundation (ALF) serves as umbrella for the organizations supporting 12 Maine lighthouses; its website, lighthousefoundation.org, is a place to check the current schedule of open house days at Rockland's two distinctive lights—Owls Head (1825) and the Rockland Breakwater Light (1827), both accessible by land. Moving east along the coast, Fort Point Light, 3 miles off Rt. 1 at Stockton Springs, and Bass Harbor Head Light, off Rt. 102 in Bass Harbor on Mount Desert, are easily accessible by land. The 1858 West Quoddy Head Light

(westquoddy.com) in Lubec, the easternmost light station in the United States, is in a class of its own. While the candy-striped light itself is open only occasionally, it's extremely photogenic and the museum in the former keeper's house doubles as the area's information center; the surrounding state park offers a stunning shore path and picnic facilities. On Campobello Island, accessed by bridge from Lubec, East Quoddy Head Lighthouse (cam pobello.com/lighthouse) is the pot of gold at the end of any East Coast lighthouse trail. Said to be the most photographed light in Canada, where it's known as Head Harbour Lighthouse, the white wooden tower is emblazoned with a red cross down its center. It's part of a full light station that fills a small island just offshore, accessible at low tide but a deadly crossing once the tide comes surging in through this

The Nubble Light, York Beach   Christina Tree

Monhegan Light

Christina Tree

narrow channel. Volunteers are on hand in-season to assist visitors. This is a great whale-watching spot.

When it comes to island lighthouses, Monhegan Island Light, capping the highest point of the island, is the most popular to visit. Its Keeper's House is now the seasonal Monhegan Museum (207-596-7003), displaying outstanding art as well as island memorabilia. Grindle Point Light on Islesboro, Burnt Harbor Light on Swan's Island, and Brown's Head Light on Vinalhaven are also easily accessible, although not open to the public.

Several light stations on small, otherwise uninhabited islands, now welcome visitors via excursions. Wood Island Lighthouse (woodislandlighthouse.org) off Biddeford Pool is occasionally open this way. At Burnt Island Light Station (lighthouse.cc/burntisland) in Boothbay Harbor, accessible by excursion boat, guides dress as lighthouse keepers from the 1950s and show visitors how life was lived on an isolated island. Other popular excursions to lights include the vintage-1795 Seguin Island Light Station (seguinisland.org) at the mouth of the Kennebec River and Little River Light (lighthousefoundation.org), sited on an island at the head of Cutler Harbor, open to the public both for day trips and overnights. It's also possible to spend the night at Goose Rocks Lighthouse (beaconpreservation.org), a freestanding spark-plug-style light in the Fox Islands Thorofare between Vinalhaven and North Haven.

Check visitmaine.com for more lighthouse information and for details about open houses.

The big Lighthouse Weekend on which many lights open to visitors is held annually in mid-September.

Sense of Place

NATURAL AND HUMAN HISTORY

Nothing is still where land meets water. In the course of a minute, grains of sand swirl, snails creep, a clam digs out of sight. In the course of an eon the whole landscape goes through revolutions.

THE DROWNED COAST

Look down in front of your feet when you stand on Cadillac Mountain, in Acadia National Park, and you can see grooves and indentations in the rock where a mile-thick layer of ice dragged itself and its load of stone and sand across the granite, heading south, until a shift in the climate melted it away. Little more than 10,000 years ago the glaciers made their final retreat, leaving behind enough sand and gravel to build Interstate 95 and thousands of other roads and buildings. They also dropped "erratic" boulders, stray giant rocks that you can see all over the coast: along Rt. 1 north of Machias, along hiking trails in the woods of Camden Hills, and on the side of South Bubble Rock, where a famous one is named Balance Rock.

Rivers created sand in front of the retreating glaciers, cut valleys out of the softer rock, and sorted the glacial till, carrying the fine sand down to the edge of the sea and sending the silt farther. Georges Bank, historically one of the finest fishing grounds in the world, sits on a bed of glacial silt and clay, and was itself once the extreme limit of the glacier that covered New England. The deep and enormous load of ice pushed the surface of the earth down underneath it. As the ice melted, the sea rose above the land, cresting 400 feet higher than it is today, and the coast was underwater. Then the earth moved upward, lifting itself out of the sea. Old deltas are now far from water, leaving curiosities like the Desert of Maine in Freeport, where overgrazing has exposed an old seashore, along with the vast, undulating blueberry barrens of Washington County.

The earth is now sinking slightly in the southern and northern tips of Maine, and the sea has been rising, 6 feet in the last 3,000 years. The coastline changes all the time under the relentless action of the sea.

The region's first men and women arrived even before the last glaciers had receded from northern Maine. They hunted woolly mammoths, bison, and caribou in a tundra-like landscape. An excellent exhibit, 12,000 Years in Maine, in the Maine State Museum (mainestatemuseum.org) in Augusta depicts the distinct periods in this history and features the Red Paint People, named for the red pigments found sprinkled in their burial sites. They flourished between 5,000 and 3,800 years ago and are believed to have harpooned swordfish from large, seaworthy boats. Displays from this period in the Robert Abbe Museum (abbemuseum.org) on Mount Desert include awls, pear-shaped net weights, and weights for sophisticated "atlatl" spears. Dioramas depict 17th-century Penobscots skillfully adjusting to the vagaries of local climate: camping at waterfalls in autumn to catch migrating salmon, moving farther inland to their birch-covered lodges in winter, back down to sheltered coves in spring and to islands such as Mount Desert in summer. Sketches and notes from a 1604 expedition by Samuel de Champlain depict, by contrast, more settled Indian villages with cultivated gardens along Maine's southern coast, west of the Kennebec River.

Maine's coastal people had this continent's earliest dealings with Europeans, who, it seems, made a nasty impression from the start. A number of Natives were kidnapped and brought back to both France and England as trophies. Via the wide tribal trading network, word got around, engendering hostilities that contributed to the failure of the 1607 Popham Colony at the mouth of the Kennebec.

Early voyagers noted distinct tribes and estimated the total number of Native people living in present-day Maine at around 40,000. The French were unquestionably better at dealings with Maine tribes than the English, thanks in part to the work of Jesuits who established missions such as that at Mount Desert. These were, however, destroyed by the English. Tribes were soon caught up in hostilities between the European contenders for trade and territory, but it was sickness, especially smallpox and plague, carried by the intruders that decimated Native communities. Perhaps 75 percent of the Native population died by the year 1616. In 1701, faced with aggressive expansion by the English colonists, the Penobscot, Passamaquoddy, Maliseet, and Micmac tribes formalized a council known as the Wabenaki (People of the Dawn) Confederacy.

During the Revolution the Micmacs and Maliseets made the unlucky choice of siding with the Crown; after the war they fled to Canada. That left only the Penobscots and Passamaquoddies, who despite fighting with the colonists were made wards of the Commonwealth. The Penobscots were confined to a reservation at Old Town,

An exhibit at the Maine State Museum traces the history of humans in Maine.

Christina Tree

near Bangor, and the Passamaquoddies to another at Perry, near Eastport. In 1786 the Penobscots deeded most of Maine to Massachusetts in exchange for 140 small islands in the Penobscot River, and in 1818 Massachusetts agreed to pay them an assortment of trinkets for the land. When Maine became a state in 1820, a trust fund was set up for the tribe, but ended up in the general treasury.

In 1957 Native Americans in Maine were allowed to vote in national elections, and not until 1967 were they allowed to vote in state elections. Never mind that a 1928 bill made all Native Americans U.S. citizens. In 1977 the Penobscot, Passamaquoddy, and Maliseet Indians sued the state, claiming that all treaties granting land to Maine were null and void, because Congress never ratified them. They asked for $25 billion and 12.5 million acres of land. In 1980 they received a settlement of $81.5 million, but no land. The money has been invested in a variety of enterprises. The Abbe Museum (abbemuseum.org) in Bar Harbor showcases the cultures of Maine's present Wabenaki, the less than 7,000 members of the Penobscot, Passamaquoddy, Micmac, and Maliseet tribes who presently live in the state. The Passamquoddy reservation (wabanaki.com) is the site of Indian Ceremonial Days in mid-August.

The Wabenaki are currently less involved in the state's flourishing tourism industry than they were in the 19th century, when they were sought-after hunting, fishing, and seagoing canoe guides and sold their stunning "fancy work" to summer tourists. The Maine Indian Basketmakers Alliance (maineindianbaskets.org) sponsors a July festival in Bar Harbor.

A LITTLE-KNOWN HISTORY

Maine's history is far too rich to begin to do it justice here. However, it's worth a try because so little of it is general knowledge—and because it's shaped so much of the Maine we see today.

By the 1500s European fishermen were harvesting cod from the abundant waters of Georges Bank, establishing fishing and trading stations including the one on Monhegan from which the Pilgrims secured food to see them through their first winters. Some of these outposts evolved into year-round trading centers such as Pemaquid (friendsofcolonialpemaquid.org), where excavations and a small museum suggest life circa 1630–50.The Pilgrims subsequently established their own Maine trading posts and, through the sale of beaver skins, were able to pay off their debt to the London merchants who financed their colony.

The first permanent European settlements in Maine were at Agamenticus (present-day York) in 1624. King Charles I of England, assuming it was his to give, gave all of Maine west of the Kennebec River to a British speculator from Plymouth, Sir Ferdinando Gorges, in 1639, directing that Gorge's portion of the mainland be named "Province or Country of Maine." Gorges chose Agamenticus, which he renamed "Georgeana," as the capital of his domain, but the ship on which he was to set sail was wrecked in the launching. This Don Quixote of Maine had to content himself with staying home and drawing up plans for an elaborate government. In 1640 the town boasted 43 officials, more than half its population. Through unlucky politics, Gorges wound up in prison, dying in 1647. In 1677 Massachusetts secured clear title to present-day Maine west of the Kennebec River.

Fort William Henry, originally built in 1692, was reconstructed in 1908 at Popham Beach.

Christina Tree

Uneasy relations between the French and English continued for years before formal war was declared. The Maine coast, particularly east of the Penobscot River, was in fairly constant dispute. Maine was heavily involved in the series of raids and retaliations remembered as the French and Indian Wars (1675–1760), a period recalled at the reconstructed English Fort William Henry (friendsof colonialpemaquid.org) in Pemaquid. Following the defeat of the French at Quebec in 1759, English colonists began to settle on the coast in larger numbers. The Museums of York (oldyork.org) suggest life during Maine's brief, peaceful colonial period. Throughout the 18th century, Maine was part of Massachusetts, the only colony with an attached but noncontiguous "district."

THE REVOLUTION

While Bostonians threw tea into the harbor, a Falmouth (present-day Portland) mob seized the Imperial tax stamps in 1765. Zealous Maine patriots claimed the first naval victory of the war when colonists captured the British cutter *Margaretta* in Machias Bay in 1775, a battle James Fenimore Cooper called the "Lexington of the seas." The first colonial warship, *Ranger*, was built at Kittery in 1777.

During the Revolution, Mainers refused to ship their highly prized white pine masts to the British fleet. The Royal Navy bombarded Falmouth and burned much of it to the ground. The British established a naval base at Castine on Penobscot Bay with an eye to making eastern Maine into a Crown colony named New Hibernia. The area attracted hundreds of loyalist families. In 1779 the Commonwealth of Massachusetts sent a fleet of 18 armed vessels and 24 transports with 1,000 troops and 400 marines to capture Castine. There the unimpressive British Fort George was manned by just 750 soldiers, with two sloops as backup. The Massachusetts forces managed to disgrace themselves miserably, hanging around long enough for several British men-of-war to come along and attack them. The surviving patriots had to walk back to Boston, and many of their officers, Paul Revere included, were court-martialed for their part in the disgrace. No thanks to Massachusetts efforts, the 1783 Treaty of Paris established Maine's present easterly border at the St. Croix River.

The British didn't relinquish Castine until 1784, at which point loyalist families moved just across Passamaquoddy Bay from Eastport to New Brunswick. Some dismantled their Castine houses, reconstructing them in St. Andrews, where they stand today.

STATEHOOD

After the Revolution, Maine prospered and grew. It became a center for production of lumber for houses, barrels, and masts. Ships from safe harbors established trade routes around the world. At the same time, impoverished and land-hungry settlers flooded into the District of Maine, doubling and redoubling the population. In contrast with other parts of New England, where Revolutionary War veterans were rewarded for military service with land or otherwise encouraged to settle, here they found themselves treated as squatters and asked to pay rent to "proprietors" who claimed vast tracts of land, largely through titles still based on grants from King George.

Revolutionary War hero General Henry Knox became a notorious proprietor. He married the granddaughter of Samuel Waldo, the Boston developer who owned most of the Midcoast area that's now Waldo County. In 1794 he built Montpelier (knoxmuseum.org), an elaborate, outsized mansion, in Thomaston (it was reconstructed as make-work project during the Depression and welcomes visitors today). These land barons assumed that they could make a killing off Maine's population surge, but their greedy plan backfired. As population grew, so did anger at the unfair demands of absentee landlords; their surveyors and rent collectors were increasingly harassed and driven off. Eventually, thanks to political pressure, an 1808 law enabled settlers to buy land on reasonable terms.

And still Massachusetts continued to treat Maine indifferently. Bay State Federalists were strongly opposed to the War of 1812, which blockaded their lucrative maritime trade. They profited hugely from the war through privateering and surreptitiously cooperated with the enemy. The British again occupied eastern Maine in 1814, capturing Machias, burning Belfast, and reoccupying Castine. A few forts, notably Edgecomb at Wiscasset, were financed locally, but Massachusetts contributed nothing. This fueled outrage against the mother state, which began to fear that Maine voters could rock the Federalist status quo.

On March 25, 1820, Maine became the 23rd state in the Union. The separation papers from Massachusetts were signed at the Jamestown Tavern in Freeport (the tavern still operates today down the street from L.L. Bean). The new status, however, seemed to help little when its Canadian boundary was disputed in 1839. Ignored by Washington, the timber-rich new state took matters into its own hands by arming its northern forts. An 1842 treaty formally ended the war, but the new state went ahead and built massive Fort Knox at the mouth of the Penobscot anyway, just in case.

At the center of the Maine State Seal stands a pine tree, signifying the tall white pines, unbroken by years of coastal wind and storms, that were coveted by the earliest explorers and subsequently turned into magnificent masts for generations of sailing ships. (A stand of century-old white pine graces the campus of Bowdoin College in Brunswick.)

By 1850 Maine was considered the shipbuilding capital of America. In Bath it's claimed that some 5,000 ships have been built along the long tidal reach of the Kennebec River. The state's golden age of shipbuilding and sail is dramatized here in the Maine Maritime Museum (mainemaritimemuseum.org).

Men of Searsport didn't just build ships, they built them to sail themselves. By 1845 the little town had constructed 99 vessels, including a full-rigged clipper; by 1860, 10 percent of the nation's deepwater shipmasters lived in Searsport. Their handsome homes still line Rt. 1 (some are now B&Bs), and their reunions in far-flung ports are chronicled in Searsport's Penobscot Marine Museum (penobscot marinemuseum.org). By 1860 one-fifth of the state's population were mariners, 759 of them masters of ships.

Although fishermen first discovered eastern Maine, they never settled there. Maine's first settlers were farmers; fishing didn't become a significant part of the economy until the 1830s, when the incoming human tide reached down east to present-day Hancok and Washington Counties. At the time Congress also granted fishermen a bounty for catching cod—which, when salted, was hugely popular with the burgeoning immigrant populations in coastal cities as well as southern and Caribbean plantations. As Colin Woodward notes in *The Lobster Coast*, the majority of these fishing schooners were owned by their captains, and crew members often held shares. Mackerel became another important catch, especially down east around Lubec and Eastport. By 1860 Maine claimed more full-time fishermen than any other state.

Maine's unlikeliest industry was ice. Massachusetts resident Frederick Tudor pioneered the concept of exporting ice from New England ponds to warmer climes but, as ski-area operators have since discovered, Maine temperatures fall below freezing more often than those in the Bay State. Tudor built vast icehouses on

The Lewis R. French, launched in 1871 in Christmas Cove, is the oldest Windjammer in America.

Fred LeBlanc, courtesy of Maine Windjammer Association

Maine State Seal

the Kennebec, creating another lucrative cargo for Maine schooners. (The small, commercial Thompson Ice House has been preserved as a museum on Rt. 129 in South Bristol.)

The Civil War had a profound effect on Maine, despite the absence of any shots fired on Maine soil. Confederate ships blocked and seized cargo vessels, and a large percentage of the seaworthy population marched off to war, many not to return. After the war, with the nation focused on westward and railroad expansion, Maine's once-crucial sea-lanes were backroaded. New government policies, moreover, decimated the state's fishing fleet.

In the 1870s through the 1890s foreign stonecutters flocked to Stonington and offshore islands like Vinalhaven, supplying the granite to build many of our most famous buildings and bridges. During this period Bath shipyards turned out Down Easters, a compromise between the clipper ship and the old-style freighter that plied the globe, and numerous shipyards produced big multimasted schooners designed to ferry coal and lime. Canneries also proliferated, processing lobster and clams as well as herring and sardines. Eventually, however, refrigeration supplanted the need for ice, granite was replaced by cement, and canned fish were replaced by frozen. Life along Maine's once-prosperous coast became increasingly challenging, and many of its more enterprising residents left.

THE IMAGE

Tourism has always been driven by images. In the 1840s Thomas Cole and Frederic Church painted scenes of Mount Desert. Etchings and sketches in the era's many papers, magazines, and children's books by lesser-known artists began projecting coastal Maine as a romantic, remote destination. After the Civil War, Maine tourism boomed. Via railroad and steamboat, residents of cities throughout the East and Midwest streamed into the Pine Tree State, many toting guidebooks published by rail and steamboat lines to boost business. Developers were

State of Maine was one of many passenger steamers that ferried tourists from points south. Courtesy, Maine Maritime Museum

quick to claim that Mount Desert Island's thick fogs were "as healthy for the body as basking in the sun."

All along the coast and on dozens of islands from Passamaquoddy to Casco Bay, hotels of every size were built, some by Boston developers but most by Maine natives. As urban factories were forced to close due to heat, vacations became an option for more and more people, not just academics and the rich. Blue-collar workers came by trolley to religious camp meetings at Old Orchard Beach and York Beach along the South Coast, where previously ignored sands were backed by new developments.

It was during this period that "summer residents" reached numbers large enough to affect both the Maine economy and culture. A breed as much apart from the transient tourist as from the local resident, these folks built seasonal homes. Initially they were people with modest incomes who built modest shingled cottages. They were later joined by many of the era's wealthiest families, who built vast summer mansions, also usually shingled and "rustic" in decor. Summer colonies mushroomed from Kennebunkport to Hancock Point and on down to Campobello Island. More than 200 lavish summer "cottages" were built in Bar Harbor, where a cadre of influential summer residents amassed 11,000 acres and persuaded the federal government to accept it in 1919 as the core of Acadia, the first national park east of the Mississippi.

World War I, coinciding with the proliferation of the Model A, brought an abrupt end to Maine's first tourism boom. The 1922 founding of the Maine Publicity Bureau (the present Maine Tourism Association), we suspect, reflects the panic of hoteliers. Then came the Depression. Over the next decades most of the island and coastal summer hotels went the way of coastal passenger boats and trains. "Motorists" stuck to motor courts and motels along Rt. 1, the tourist trail.

In 1947 much of Bar Harbor was destroyed in a forest fire. The French paper *Le Figaro* reported that the peasants of Maine had struck a blow against feudalism. The town's year-round residents did not like being called peasants. The fact is that Maine's wealthy summer residents prided themselves on their relationships with locals. Over pie and coffee, yachtsmen and lobstermen talked politics, weather, and boats. Summer residents embraced the romantic image of coastal Maine as a throwback to simpler times. The fact that "natives" came of sturdy European stock like themselves reinforced this image—which persists.

By the 1960s much of the coast had dropped off the tourist map. Gradually, over the next few decades, surviving summer hotels were restored as inns or condominiums. Bed & breakfasts began appearing in the 1980s, transforming former sea captains' homes and summer mansions into B&Bs, in the process reopening to visi-

The Claremont Hotel in Southwest Harbor, painted in 1885 by Xanthus Smith

Courtesy, The Claremont Hotel

Summer season garden party in York, 1884
Photograph by Frederick Quimby, courtesy, Museums of Old York

tors corners on the peninsulas, islands, and other off-the-beaten-track places.

For decades Acadia National Park was a public toehold in the mostly privately owned coast, but thanks to both state programs and private land trusts, coastal preserves are steadily increasing, largely through contributions of land and funds from third- and fourth-generation "summer residents," many of whom now live in Maine year-round.

It's also now easier than ever for casual visitors to get out on the water, the only way to really appreciate the beauty of this coast. The Maine Windjammer fleet (sailmaine.org), originally introduced in the '30s, has been reestablished and expanded, offering affordable multiday sailing cruises on traditional coastal schooners in Penobscot Bay. Kayaking outfitters introduce thousands each summer to the delights of paddling along quiet coves or out to islands, observing seals and waterfowl close up. Whale-watching expeditions also lure landlubbers, along with an ever-increasing number of excursion boats.

Maine coastal landscape has been shaped as much by tourism as by other forces in the state's history. In the 19th century summer visitors, including *Atlantic Monthly* editor William Dean Howells and Sam Clemens (Mark Twain), were responsible for restoring York's colonial buildings. Portland's Old Port, too, has been revitalized by catering to visitors—and where would L.L. Bean and all the Freeport outlets be without shoppers from away? On down the coast through Boothbays' busy waterfront, Rockland's galleries, and Camden's and Bar Harbor's teeming main shops and restaurants, it's difficult to overstate the impact of tourism on this "Vacationland."

According to recent research, roughly 80 percent of Maine's visitors return after an initial visit. For many there is a longing to belong here. An incoming tide of commuters, telecommuters, and retirees is swelling and changing Maine's population, most dramatically along the South Coast. Up and down the coast there's talk of "WOOFs" (well-off older folks), who are becoming the volunteer engines of their adopted communities.

Visitors and transplants alike need to be aware of the special, increasingly fragile sense of place each community possesses, a compound of the many generations of people who have shaped it.

Tourism continues to be driven by images. Maine's icons include lighthouses and lobster boats, schooners and weathered wharves and fishermen. Whereas in other parts of the country natural beauty is the only draw, here human-built beauty is a big part of the picture.

1

South Coast

KITTERY TO KENNEBUNK

Much of southern Maine's coastline is flat, smoother than Maine's nickname the Rocky Coast might imply. Its estuaries and strands stretch out for miles along beaches and thin woods, presenting only a few stretches of the rocky outcroppings that mark most of the Maine beaches farther north. The water's edge in York Beach, Ogunquit, and the Kennebunks mostly soothes the eye and the mind with distant vistas of ocean surf and sand.

Yet enough variety marks the landscape that artists crowd into Ogunquit in good weather to paint its picturesque Perkins Cove and other harbors. City visitors have been frequenting the expanse of Long Sands Beach in York Beach for as long as cities have persuaded people to leave. And the heightened coastline in Kennebunkport, where rocks rise up out of the sea near Walker Point—the famous summer home of former president George H. W. Bush—endows the big summer houses there with drama and glamour that visitors to Cape Arundel Inn can take in on an overnight visit.

Every one of these communities is busy and sometimes jammed at the height of summer. Fall and late spring are preferable times for a visit, so long as the beach is not the only reason you come. And though the beaches are sublime, hiking, biking, golfing, and kayaking in a wet suit extend the season. You certainly won't have to worry about finding a good meal, with restaurants open year-round that are renowned for the quality of their meals: Anneke Jans, Arrows, Joshua's, Angelina's, and 98 Provence.

The Yorks and Kittery

Check out these great attractions and activities . . .

Kittery's village, a small, historic spot at the southernmost tip of Maine's coast, is hard to find from I-95, Exit 3, where Rt. 1 is lined with familiar outlet stores well loved by shoppers.

But you'll also find unusual stores that might appeal if you're looking for things truly out of the ordinary. The Kittery Trading Post (207-439-2700; kitterytradingpost.com; Rt. 1) is a huge store that

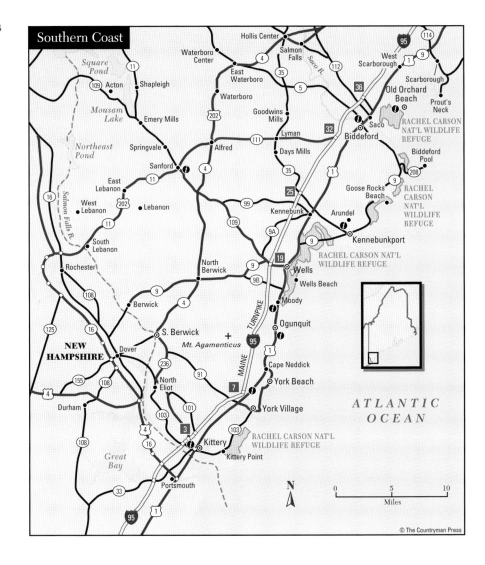

© The Countryman Press

some people make a destination, full of sporting gear, shoes, and sportswear, and offering legendary end-of-summer sales.

For exquisite antique quilts and antique fabrics, many quilters and collectors seek out the unique **Rocky Mountain Quilts** (207-363-6800; rockymountainquilts .com; 130 York St., York Village), run by Betsey Telford-Goodwin, a scholar of the craft.

Anyone hungry for lunch or dinner should consider taking Exit 2, traveling to Rt. 1 avoiding the underpass, and heading south to Wallingford Square and the small area around Rt. 1 where high-quality food shops and restaurants cluster. The geography of the state of Maine suitably begins with some exciting meals. You

Long Sands Beach, York Beach   Nancy English

might stop at Loco Coco's Tacos (207-438-9322; locococos.com; 36 Walker St., Kittery) for a poblano chili stuffed with queso blanco, which you could enjoy on the terrace or take to go. Down Gerrish Island Lane and at the end of Pocahontas Rd., Fort Foster Park offers a place for a picnic and a walk on trails and beaches.

Wallingford Square is a good spot to wind up for dinner because Anneke Jans (207-439-0001; annkejans.net; 60 Wallingford Square, Kittery) serves fantastic bistro meals that might start with Bangs Island mussels finished with blue cheese and cream or fried olives; then go on to pan-roasted trout with potato chorizo hash. But call ahead for a reservation. In 2010 the bistro's owners opened AJ's Wood Grill Pizza (207-439-9700; ajswoodgrillpizza.com; 68 Wallingford Square, Kittery) in the same building, serving organic, seven-grain dough that's grilled first on a wood-fired grill then topped with grilled vegetables and more and finished in the oven. It's open daily.

Bob's Clam Hut on Rt. 1 is a good spot for fried clams, and picnic tables in the back of the building allow outdoor dining in good weather. A good spot for sandwiches is in York Village at The Rowan Street Café (207-363-2035; 241 York St.).

Behind Frisbee's 1828 Market on Rt. 103 is a lonely tombstone marking the burial place of Colonel William Pepperell—who was born in Devonshire, England, in 1646 and died in Kittery in 1734—and his son Sir William Pepperell, who defeated the French at the Louisburg fortress in Nova Scotia. His widow built the 1760 house next to the 1730 First Congregational Church, Maine's oldest church, and both compel attention.

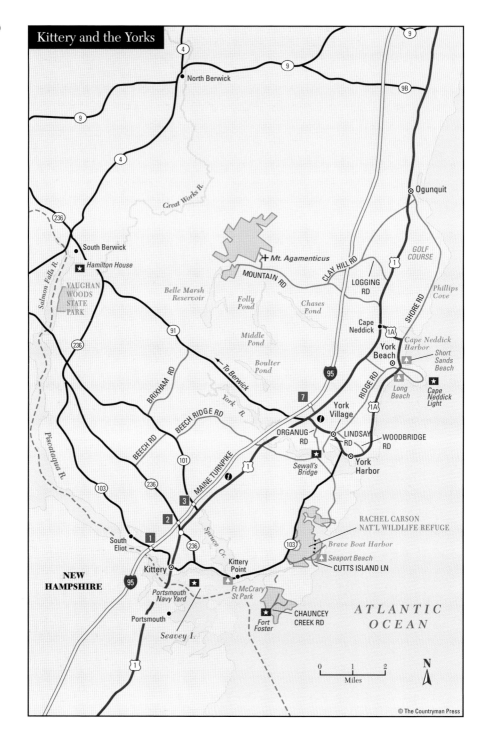

Kittery and the Yorks

Down Chauncey Creek Rd. in summer you are likely to encounter a traffic jam outside the Chauncey Creek Lobster Pound (207-439-1030; chaunceycreek .com; 16 Chauncey Creek Rd., Kittery Point). This would be the first spot a tourist entering Maine could go to really satisfy the requirements of a good lobster dinner, which to our minds involves setting just as much as steamed lobster. The outdoor seating, some picnic tables sheltered from the rain but none heated, overlooks the tidal Chauncey Creek. BYOB.

A geographic introduction is key to navigating the sprawl of the Yorks, four loosely connected villages that stretch many miles from the surf off York Beach inland to Cape Neddick. York Village and York Harbor lie at the southern end of the area and are not immediately encountered when you leave I-95 at Exit 7. Still, that exit does put you right in front of the driveway to Stonewall Kitchen (800-826-1752; stonewallkitchen.com/cafe.html), a delightful food emporium and café that's the company store for a business that began with some pots of homemade jam.

If you would like to get out of the car and stretch your legs far from the popular places, head inland. Trails lace the woods of Mount Agamenticus, maintained by the Agamenticus Conservation Region (agamenticus.org). The trails can be used by bicylists, hikers, and equestrians, but the summit is marred with cell phone antennas and buildings. Still, you can climb up to an open perch and turn your back to the commercial detritus while you count the passing hawks during fall migration.

This wooded area is home to spotted turtles—with lovely yellow dots on their top shells—as well as other turtles, some threatened. Watch out for them crossing the road from spring to midfall but especially in May and June. The females are seeking higher ground to lay their eggs, but many are killed before they reach it. (If you find an injured turtle, call the Center for Wildlife in York at 207-361-1400 to find a licensed rehabilitator.)

The ocean walk many will prefer is Cliff Path and Fisherman's Walk, which holds a charming passage along a little suspension bridge called Wiggly Bridge,

Long Sands Beach, York Beach

Nancy English

built in the 1930s. In York Harbor village by the George Marshall Store can be found the easiest-accessed beginning point of the 1-mile walk that takes you through Steedman Woods. A stretch along Rt. 103 takes you to a parking circle at York Harbor beach, between York Harbor Inn and Stage Neck Inn, where the beach path can be rough. Then you double back.

The Museums of Old York (207-363-4974; oldyork.org) include eight historic buildings. A visit starts with an orientation film in the visitors center, a reconstructed 1830s barn attached to Jeffers' Tavern, built in 1754. The old Gaol was the only jail for the whole of the province of Maine until 1760, and parts of it date to 1719; female immates' stories in the dismal cells make the visit memorable. A chandlery, a finely furnished 1730 house, a farm laborer's house, and a schoolhouse are other distinguished parts of this complex, open from early June through Columbus Day weekend, Mon.–Sat. 10–5.

Nubble Light is a photogenic lighthouse just offshore near Long Sands Beach in York Beach with a parking lot for its many visitors. What's more, it's close to Brown's Ice Cream (207-363-1277; 232 Nubble Rd., York Beach), just west of Rt. 1A and an essential stop whatever the season.

Checking In

Best places to stay in the Yorks and Kittery

Dockside Guest Quarters (207-363-2868; docksidegq.com; 22 Harris Island Rd., York) is one of our favorite family-run inns, with a view of the harbor outlet from a handsome old house and four modern cottages. All 25 rooms and

Nubble Light, York Beach

Nancy English

Brown's Ice Cream, York Beach   Nancy English

renovated, spic-and-span rooms with Maine-cottage-style furniture. On the second floor is the restaurant Blue Sky (207-363-0050; blueskyonyorkbeach .com), where you can count on oysters Rockefeller and a good steak.

Smaller, more economical and intimate lodgings start with The Morning Glory Inn (207-363-2062; morning gloryinnmaine.com; 129 Seabury Rd., York), where Bonnie and Bill Alston provide a welcome, a flower garden, and an oasis of peace that visitors love. This is a bed & breakfast with three charming bedrooms; a full breakfast is included in the rates.

The Inn at Harmon Park (207-363-2031) is in walking distance of the harbor in an 1899 Victorian, and it's the least expensive of the lodgings we mention while still equal in hospitality and most amenities. Here Sue Antal offers B&B Sept.–May, a weekly rental in summer.

In Kittery, The Portsmouth Harbor Inn and Spa (207-439-4040; innat portsmouth.com; 6 Water St., Kittery), an 1890s redbrick inn, stands just off the Kittery green and steps from a smaller bridge spanning the Piscataqua River. Guests can walk to New Hampshire's lively downtown Portsmouth from this inn for dinner or shopping, after enjoying some of the services offered at the spa, perhaps the seacoast lavender sugar scrub, exfoliation, and light massage.

lodgings enjoy a water view. Fishing equipment, bicycles, and even Boston Whalers are available to guests. Breakfasts with egg dishes and homemade rolls and muffins are just the beginning.

If you're a tennis lover, The Stage Neck Inn (207-363-3850; stageneck .com; 8 Stage Neck Rd., York Harbor) offers tennis courts along with its outdoor pool, rooms with all the amenities, many with a water view, and a good restaurant. The bar downstairs might be even more congenial, with woodworking details that mimic the inside of a finely built sailing ship.

Right in the middle of the village of York Beach, The Atlantic House (207-363-0051; atlantichouseyork beach.com; 2 Beach St.) holds newly

Ogunquit and Wells

Check out these great attractions and activities . . .

Ogunquit became famous as an artists' colony by the turn of the last century, and that legacy can be enjoyed in the excellent collection of more than 1,600 modern artworks owned by the Ogunquit Museum of American Art (207-646-4909; ogunquitmuseum.org; 543 Shore Rd., Ogunquit) from mid-May to October. Opened in 1953, the museum is set on a ledge overlooking the ocean, and its 3-acre garden is a fine spot to enjoy peace and quiet. Turning its gaze onto

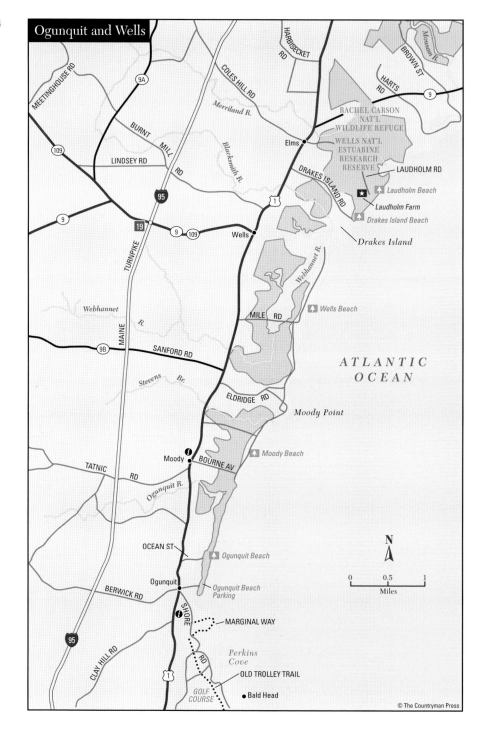

Ogunquit and Wells

its immediate past, the museum's exhibits show off Ogunquit's art colony history and the roots of the Ogunquit Art Association. Works by Marsden Hartley, John Marin, Charles Burchfield, Wolf Kahn, and Marguerite and William Zorach, along with the large, forceful wooden sculptures standing outside by Bernard Langlais, are just a tiny few of the possibilities visitors will encounter.

Walking is the best way to get to know Ogunquit, and its lovely Marginal Way is the most scenic of its many walking trails. The trail hugs the shore and is set on rocky outcroppings south of Ogunquit Beach to Oarweed Cove, where walkers emerge into the lively (if not mobbed) area called Perkins Cove. It's cheaper to walk there than to pay for pricey parking, and you can climb into a free trolley outside many of the area's motels and inns to reach one end or the other of the walk.

Walking right at water's edge is likely the most popular way to enjoy Ogunquit's 3.5-mile expanse of white sand, set in a long neck beside the Ogunquit River and running parallel to the town.

The Carson Interpretive Trail, 1 mile long, is part of the Rachel Carson National Wildlife Refuge, which has 10 different sites along the South Coast. It's open sunrise to sunset. Seats are provided at viewing stations along this level, short trail, located off Rt. 9 just south of the Kennebunk line in Wells.

Carson Interpretive Trail, Wells   Nancy English

Next door is the Wells National Estuarine Research Reserve at Laudholm Farm (207-646-1555; wellsreserve.org; just off Rt. 9). Comprising more than 2,000 acres of estuary, the reserve hold meadows and two barrier beaches once part of Laudholm Farm, a saltwater farm started in the 1640s and active until the 1980s. Now birders seek out the 7 miles of trails and protected coastline. Fiddle playing and pumpkin rolling are part of a popular festival called Punkinfiddle (punkin fiddle.org) held the last Saturday of September.

Rt. 1 through Ogunquit and north to Wells and the Shore Rd. south to Perkins Cove are lined with lodgings and restaurants. Traffic often proceeds at a crawl. Some visitors like to stay close to the village of Ogunquit so they can walk to dinner, to the beach, and back to their rooms, with an assist from the free trolley. Nightlife in Ogunquit in summer is one the area's popular features. Many others flock to see *The Judy Show* at The Front Porch (207-646-4005; thefrontporch .net; 9 Shore Rd.), right smack in the middle of Ogunquit. The show is performed by Michael Holmes, who has presented it here for more than 10 years and tours in the off-season. His parody of Judy Garland is based on Garland's 1964 TV show; he also brings other star impersonations to the stage while he sings and entertains in glamorous costumes.

Musicians perform original numbers at Jonathans (207-646-4777; jonathans restaurant.com; 92 Bourne Lane, Ogunquit), which is also quite a good restaurant. Reserve tickets in advance for the often sold-out shows, perhaps presenting long-time star Richie Havens; Shawn Colvin, a contemporary folk musician who has won three Grammy Awards; or singer-songwriter Nanci Griffith.

Ogunquit Playhouse (207-646-5511; ogunquitplayhouse.org; 10 Main St., Ogunquit) has roots in the 1930s and the Little Theater Movement that planted theaters in small towns. The theater in Ogunquit was built in 1937 by Walter and Maude Hartwig, who started their own Manhattan Theatre colony in Ogunquit and hired stars like Ethel Barrymore to perform in summer. Sally Struthers was a 2007 star in *The Full Monty*, and every summer the playhouse continues to present professional theater.

Checking In

Best places to stay in Ogunquit and Wells

Beachmere Inn (207-646-2231; beach mereinn.com; 62 Beachmere Place, Ogunquit) has been run by the women of the same family since 1937. It has undergone extensive renovation and rebuilding while continuing to enjoy a secluded location on the edge of the sea and proximity to the village of Ogunquit. Marginal Way is accessible through a gate in the lawn. Spacious accommodations emphasize function and beauty almost equally, with locally made, elegant furniture, kitchenettes, some gas fireplaces and a few wood-burning fireplaces, and of course wonderful views. A pub with a light-fare menu makes it possible to stay on the grounds, wandering from the oceanside to the green lawn and to the sauna, for days on end.

On one hot August Wednesday, owner and innkeeper Bruce Senecal—who runs Gazebo Inn (207-646-3733; gazeboinnogt.com; 572 Main St., Rt. 1, Ogunquit) with Scott Osgood—told us he'd already turned away 600 people, and it was only 1 PM! Make reservations early to be sure of a room at this well-run, affordable, and convenient bed & breakfast. The modern rooms have all the requisites while the business retains a comfortable intimacy and welcome. Breakfast is stupendous, and a movie room with cushy couches along with a bar, outdoor pool, gym, sauna, and massage room keep the social scene lively. Footbridge Beach, away from the crowds and across Ogunquit River, is a short hike away. Osgood and Senecal also own 2 Village Square Inn (207-646-5779; 2vsquare .com; 14 Village Square Lane, Ogunquit) and Admiral's Quarters (207-646-3733; captainogt.com; Rt. 1, Ogunquit), across from the Ogunquit Lobster Pound. Pets can visit the suites at Admiral's Quarters, where rooms with kitchens and kitchenettes and lower weekly rates can make a visit economical.

Just south of Perkins Cove, The Riverside Motel (207-646-2741; river sidemotel.com; 50 Riverside Lane) offers basic, clean, and comfortable accommodations right in the heart of things. The rooms overlook the water, but the location keeps rates high in August. Another lodging with a primo location, a mile or two south of the Riverside Motel and near the border of York Beach, is Cliff House Resort & Spa (207-361-1000; cliffhousemaine .com; Shore Rd.), an elegant, historic resort with a new spa building and vanishing horizon pool that visitors can float in while staring at the vast ocean just beyond. A rocky cliff under the main building gives the setting unusual drama; the dining room is set inside with panoramic views. Gas fireplaces in some of the new rooms and indoor pools are improvements that came along after the U.S. military took over the place during World War II to use as a submarine lookout.

Listed last because it's out of town and one of our favorite places, The Beach Farm Inn (207-646-8493; beachfarminn.com; 97 Eldridge Rd., Wells) is far from the madding crowd, nicely appointed with fine furniture, some upholstered and some crafted by the innkeepers themselves, and everything as comfortable as anyone could wish. The pool is in view of the breakfast porch, where blueberry pancakes might be served; the full breakfast is included in the rates. Modest rates reflect shared and private baths, and accommodations include two cottages.

The Cliff House, Ogunquit   Nancy English

Local Flavors

The taste of Ogunquit and Wells—local restaurants, cafés, and more

Joshua's (207-646-3355; joshuas.biz; 1637 Post Rd., Rt. 1, Wells) stands at the top of the list in this region, at least as far as we're concerned, because of its excellent, uncomplicated cuisine founded on fresh produce, much of it grown at the owners' own farm. Duck leg confit with port sauce and rack of lamb are two standards of excellence on the menu.

With its elaborate invention and exquisite service, Arrows (207-361-1100; arrowsrestaurant.com; 41 Berwick Rd., Cape Neddick—but most easily accessed from Ogunquit village) has been wowing customers for years. You can probably order an appetizer of osetra caviar for $150 or, somewhat more reasonably, a lobster potpie for $22, and you can be sure the salad was picked, probably in the restaurant's own garden, that day. Tasting menus offer the full array of creativity in the kitchen, and cost $95–135 in 2010, but a Friday $39 three-course bistro dinner was also served. Owners Clark Frasier and Mark Gaier won the well-deserved Best Chef Northeast award from the James Beard Foundation in 2010. The dress code seems to have relaxed, but shorts are still not allowed on male guests (closed in winter).

The same two restaurateurs own MC Perkins Cove (207-646-6263; mcperkinscove.com; 111 Perkins Cove Rd., Ogunquit), where shorts are okay but the line is drawn at bathing suits. A bar menu with a lobster roll and french fries for $19.95 means most of us can sample the fare, and it is excellent.

Wonderful raw oysters could start a more formal meal, with bacon-wrapped meat loaf or tea-smoked duck breast with apricot and star-anise-cured confit to follow. The view of ocean waves, either crashing near the building or down the rocky beach at low tide, make the view from the tables at the windows particularly wonderful.

Angelina's Ristorante and Wine Bar (207-646-0445; angelinasogunquit.com; 655 Main St., Rt. 1, Ogunquit) does Italian classics as good as they can be. Reservations are a must at this hopping restaurant named for owner David Giarusso's grandmother. His wonderful zuppa di pesce sings with bright basil, garlic, sweet tomatoes, and fresh seafood, and the high-quality veal and beef make just as good a dish of Piccata or pizzaiola. Risottos and fresh house pasta dishes are specialties. You'll wish you were staying long enough to try a lot more on the menu than you can sample in one night—but maybe you are.

98 Provence (207-646-9898; 98provence.com; 262 Shore Rd., Ogunquit) serves cuisine from the south of France in a handsome, rustic farmhouse with an open-beam ceiling and decorative touches from Provence. Seared foie gras with apricot-fennel chutney is likely to be incredible, and if gazpacho is on the menu that will be, too. The flavors are vibrant in rabbit confit with olive oil, rosemary, preserved lemon, and garlic white bean puree; or lamb rib chops with summer savory.

Starting the day at Amore Breakfast and Café (207-646-6661; amore breakfast.com; 309 Shore Rd., Ogunquit), open 7 AM–1 PM, is a local tradition easy to observe when the menu offers bananas Foster French toast, coated with pecans and stuffed with cream cheese, or a lobster Benedict with two poached eggs and hollandaise around sautéed lobster.

For a boiled lobster, The Lobster Shack Restaurant (207-646-2941; lobster-shack.com; 110 Perkins Cove Rd., Ogunquit) does it right, with a big

sink to wash up at afterward in the dining room, and thick slab tables easy to get to work on. Lobsters, steamers, lobster stew, chowder and chili, some sandwiches, and beer round out the simple menu.

Kennebunk and Kennebunkport

Check out these great attractions and activities . . .

The Kennebunk River forms the boundary between Kennebunk and Kennebunkport, with the southern town, Kennebunk, the one you see first after exiting from the highway. The fine Main St. with brick buildings is quiet compared with the crowded sidewalks closer to the sea, where Kennebunk and Kennebunkport are connected by a little bridge over Rt. 9, with good casual restaurants like Federal Jacks—one of Maine's first brewpubs—on the Kennebunk side and Alisson's across the bridge in Kennebunkport.

But back inland for another moment, The Brick Store Museum and Archives (207-985-4802; brickstoremuseum.org; 117 Main St., Kennebunk) holds exhibits about local history and artifacts in its own historic structure, an 1825 dry-goods store built by shipowner William Lord (whose home is the Captain Lord Mansion mentioned in *Places to Stay*). The museum now fills several buildings on the block as its work has grown over the years, with exhibits, lectures, and art shows among the offerings.

The Wedding Cake House near Kennebunkport   Nancy English

The Kennebunks/
Old Orchard Beach Area

© The Countryman Press

But one of its most popular is outside the walls and down the street, on the historic walking tours that guide visitors along a mile of flat sidewalks and streets to view the Colonial, Federal, Greek Revival, Queen Anne, and Colonial Revival architectural styles magnificently preserved in Kennebunk's historic district.

On the road to Kennebunkport, The Wedding Cake House pulls in all passing eyes. Though the house is privately owned, tours were offered in the summer of 2010. Its original owner, George W. Bourne, became enamored of Milan's Gothic cathedral on his journeys, and undertook similar ornamentation of his Federal-style house in 1852 using hand tools and with the assistance of a ship carpenter's apprentice.

The Kennebunkport Historical Society (207-967-2751; kporthistory.org; 8 Maine St., Kennebunkport) presents the Greek Revival Nott House with its Doric colonnade for guided tours, showing off carpets, furniture, and wallpaper that are original to the house. A tasteful gift shop in the Carriage House sells souvenirs of gentility. Hours vary according to the season.

Christmas Prelude is a popular event in early December, opening up the Nott House up for a champagne reception while the shops keep late hours and horse-drawn carriages pass in the streets. Tree lighting, a crafts fair, and a pancake breakfast offer more ways to get in the spirit.

The Seashore Trolley Museum (207-967-2712; trolleymuseum.org; 195 Log Cabin Rd., Kennebunkport) opened in 1939 when trolley cars were seeing their days as basic mass transportation coming to an end. Today more than 250 vehicles from all corners of the world are displayed, and a 3-mile excursion comes with the price of a ticket. A locomotive engine from the Atlantic Shore Line Railway was restored after 8,000 hours of volunteer dedication; the engine was part of a York County trolley line that once covered 87 miles of track.

Checking In

Best places to stay in Kennebunk and Kennebunkport

Three historic buildings standing around a small green in Kennebunkport offer luxurious rooms. The Captain Lord Mansion (207-967-3141; captainlord.com; 6 Pleasant St., Kennebunkport) is furnished with massive beds that might come equipped with steps; one over-the-top room has a bathroom with a gas fireplace. You won't lack for comfort in these plush surroundings, and the halls and parlors are just as elegant. A full breakfast in the country kitchen is part of the rates, but the spa services are extra.

Captain Fairfield Inn (800-322-1928; captainfairfield.com; 8 Pleasant St., Kennebunkport) is a little more restrained in its decor, perhaps showing off a more austere architectural style. The room called The Library has its own private porch. But visitors to any of the rooms enjoy the perks, from the excellent breakfast to the afternoon cookies.

The Captain Jefferds Inn (207-967-2311; captainjefferdsinn.com; 5 Pearl St., Kennebunkport) has a room called the Monticello with a lace-canopied queen-sized four-poster and a gas fireplace to keep the blue-and-white color scheme warm and friendly. The more rustic decor in the carriage house could be more to many's liking, and the amenities are just as fine. "Baxter" was inspired by Maine camps—but in this case everything works and nothing leaks.

Old Fort Inn (207-967-5353; old fortinn.com; 8 Old Fort Ave., Kennebunkport) is off the main road in Kennebunkport with its own 15-acre site, worth the trouble of finding. The 16 guest rooms are handsomely lodged in a stone-and-brick carriage house, each holding its own wet bar and mini kitchen, and the tiled bathroom floors are heated. A pool, tennis court, and horseshoe pitch offer diversion, along with the fine antiques and gifts in the inn's shop.

Cape Arundel Inn (207-967-2125; capearundelinn.com; 208 Ocean Ave., Kennebunkport) has an incredibly good restaurant. Rooms in the inn and an addition all face the ocean, with big picture windows making the most of it. They're utterly comfortable and decorated imaginatively by owner Jack Nahil, who is a fine-art painter. But perhaps the most persuasive thing about him is the fact that many on his staff have worked for him for decades. His chef is one, and his restaurant is so well run, the food so outstanding, it's easy to see why employee and employer would want to keep things just the way they are.

The Colony Hotel (207-967-3331; thecolonyhotel.com; 140 Ocean Ave., Kennebunkport) is the real thing, an old resort still going strong, its strengths in its good, solid furniture, and its limitations in the old style that furniture maintains. If it's pleasing to your taste, it will satisfy—and an old-fashioned place is one of our favorite things. There's a heated saltwater pool, golf, and children's activities; breakfast is included in the rates.

Tides Inn-By-the-Sea (207-967-3757; tidesinnbythesea.com; 252 Kings Hwy., Goose Rocks Beach) is another old-fashioned place, an 1899 shingle-style summer hotel designed by John Calvin Stevens with windows open to the sound of waves. Visited by Sir Arthur Conan Doyle and Theodore Roosevelt in its early days, it seems a little sleepier now—just the way you want it. Spend the day across the street on the wide sandy Goose Rocks Beach, and dine at night in the Belvidere Club Bistro. The Victorian Bar is a great place to unwind.

Seaside Inn and Cottages (207-967-4461; kennebunkbeach.com; 80 Beach Ave., Kennebunk) also enjoys a seaside location, this one south of the Kennebunk River on Kennebunk Beach. Nine generations of innkeepers have kept this property in the family, and although it has changed shape over the years the business lays claim to being the oldest inn in the country. Today the rooms are in a two-story modern building, while breakfast is served in an 1850 former boathouse. At this place you don't even have to cross the street to get to the beach, and off-season the rates are very attractive.

The Franciscan Guest House (207-967-4865; franciscanguesthouse .com; 26 Beach Ave, Kennebunk) is the most affordable lodging in this area, and if the rooms are Spartan, the Lithuanian breakfast with homemade farmer's cheese, raisin bread, carrot bread, and potato bread is not (and it's included in the rates). Shrines to the Virgin Mary and others dot the 66-acre grounds.

Down the road a bit and on the other side from the Guest House is The White Barn Inn (207-967-2321; whitebarninn.com; 37 Beach St., Kennebunk), the *ne plus ultra* in elegance. Antiques-furnished rooms have every possible amenity and more, with fresh fruit on check-in just one small detail and perhaps one small part of the 5.45 percent hospitality fee added to the steep bill. An elaborate tea is served in the afternoon to guests, and touring bikes are on offer, but spa services and the use of the yacht *True Blue* are extra.

Local Flavors

The taste of Kennebunk and Kennebunkport—local restaurants, cafés, and more

The White Barn Inn, described briefly above, is also a famous restaurant, rated 5 Diamonds by AAA and 5 Stars by *Forbes*. Set inside a barn that's filled with flowers, with tall windows inserted in handsome wood walls, this is an attractive place for a good meal—or at least we think it would be if we had the chance to eat here. We can't persuade any of our employers to pay for a meal at $98 per person plus tax and tip and wine. Ricotta cannelloni and garden vegetable frittata with candied cashews, tabouli, and wild mushrooms was an entrée on one August menu.

We could, however, pay for a lobster roll at The Ramp, the downstairs bar at Pier 77 (207-967-8500; pier77 restaurant.com; 77 Pier Rd., Cape Porpoise), and it was one of the best lobster rolls we've ever had, rich, slightly warm, utterly sensuous and fresh. Cape Porpoise is north of the village of Kennebunkport, and Pier 77 is down Pier Rd. off Rt. 9, but the place is still part of Kennebunkport. In any event, it's an exceptionally good restaurant, more formal upstairs and lively and casual down, with a few seats outside to take in the sunset and the lobster boats unloading at the dock.

Nunan's Lobster Hut (207-967-4362; 9 Mills Rd.) is in Cape Porpoise

The Ramp at Pier 77, Cape Porpoise   Nancy English

ramps; or day-boat cod chowder elaborated with fresh corn, leeks, fingerling potatoes, cream, and chives.

Nearby at Old Vines Wine Bar (207-967-2310; oldvineswinebar.com; 173 Port Rd., Lower Village, Kennebunk), owner Mike Farrell has put together a wine list that will keep you engaged and intrigued. You might also find yourself putting together a shopping list for your own cellar or kitchen cupboard. Sipping the great wines, plates of Serrano ham or house-cured duck prosciutto, cheese plates or seasonal salads—perhaps an heirloom tomato tartine spread with basil pesto and covered with melted fresh mozzarella—could keep you from leaving for dinner anywhere else.

Port Lobster (800-486-7029; port lobster.com; 122 Ocean Ave., Kennebunkport) sells cooked lobsters and lobster rolls—and since it's the source of the picked lobster meat that fills lobster rolls at most local restaurants, you might as well get the stuff fresh from the source.

Fried seafood is what Seafood Center (207-985-7391; seafoodcenter ofmaine.com; 1181 Portland Rd., Arundel) does best, and with its reputation for high-quality oil and cleanliness, you can feel almost proud to enjoy it as thoroughly as you inevitably will. The plain dining room is 1 mile north of Kennebunk on Rt. 1, open year-round to satisfy the craving for fried clams, fried scallops, and fried haddock.

The homemade ice cream at Arundel Ice Cream Shop (207-604-2734; arundelicecreamshop.com; 1185 Portland Rd.) served next door might taste best in summer. However, the place uses real whipped cream on the sundaes, quality-controlled hot fudge, and Guittard chocolate sprinkles. It looks like a visit is in order anytime at all—but call first for hours.

village, and its series of rustic rooms have been sheltering hordes of lobster lovers since 1953. (Before that customers bought their lobsters from the front yard from an open kettle, $1.25 for the first one and 80 cents for a second!) Take a number and wait outside till a table is ready. Bring cash, because the business does not accept credit cards.

Local 50 (207-985-0850; local kennebunk.com; 50 Main St., Kennebunk) embraces local produce and meats and fish in all their glory, preparing them in Asian, French, or any cuisine other that makes sense, like a seviche of striped bass with pineapple salsa, pickled chili, and corn tortillas. There's a veggie noodle bowl for vegetarians, and scallops, fish stew, steak frites, and lobster carbonara for the rest of us.

On the Marsh (207-967-2299; onthemarsh.com; 46 Western Ave., Lower Village, Kennebunkport) is a fussy restaurant overlooking a tidal marsh. Chef Jeffery Savage has perfected an elegant menu here, with local mushroom ragu on tagliatelle with wild

2

The Portland Region

INCLUDING FREEPORT

The Big City, Maine-style, is a place to explore on foot. In fact Portland's downtown is located on a foot-shaped peninsula with the Eastern Promenade, which looks out to sea, at its toe and the Western Prom on the back of the heel. Congress St. runs down the length of it. At its intersection with Forest Ave., the Arts District is in charge of filling the shop windows with art and artists' installations.

From Longfellow Square to Congress Square with the Portland Museum of Art; from City Hall and the top of Exchange Street down through the Old Port to Commercial Street—the main street of the waterfront Old Port—Portland teems with great restaurants, fine hotels, inns and B&Bs, excellent galleries, and extraordinary shops.

Easily accessible both north and south are beaches, amusement parks, and shopping destinations. Canadians have flocked to Old Orchard Beach for generations, and the beach community, now close to its own summertime train station, still thrives on visitors who love its diversions. Saco and Biddeford, historic mill towns that flank opposite sides of the Saco River, have in common a revitalized mill district with its own brewpub and restaurant.

North of Portland and just a 20-minute drive on I-295, Freeport keeps polishing its shopping luster with a new shopping complex and movie theater. L.L. Bean's giant hunting boot, outside the door of its flagship store, isn't wearing out, of course, because the business fixes it when it does—just as it does anything a customer returns. Customers enjoy the company's lifetime guarantee: Bring in worn-out boots—or anything else—for a replacement, no questions asked.

L.L. Bean's big boot, Freeport   Bill Davis

Saco, Biddeford, Old Orchard Beach, Scarborough, and Cape Elizabeth

Attractions, activities, accommodations, eateries, etc.

Saco Museum (207-283-3861; dyer librarysacomusuem.org; 371 Main St., Saco) has beefed up its exhibits, offering folk art and antiques among its permanent exhibits of paintings. Period bedchambers from both a wealthy family's house and a working-class house make historical insight vivid indeed. Just down the street is Mia's at Pepperell Square (207-284-6427; miasatpepperellsquare.com; 17 Pepperell Square, Saco), an excellent restaurant with surprising sophistication. Count on really good crabcakes, butter-poached lobster, and, perhaps, beef Stroganoff.

Cross the river south for several good eating places. On Saco Island overlooking Saco River Falls is Run of the Mill Brew Pub (207-571-9648; 100 Main St., Saco), which serves its own excellent beer and decent pub food. A seat on the patio outside would be the ticket on a summer night, the air cooled by the river alongside.

Just a bit south on Rt. 1 in Biddeford is Maine's best Indian restaurant, Jewel of India (207-282-5600; thejewelofindia.com; 26 Alfred St., Biddeford), which now has a branch in South Portland (45 Western Ave., near The Maine Mall). The fine fresh flavors of the spices and the main ingredients make this Indian restaurant stand out from the others in Maine.

Of course, lobster and fried seafood aren't far from any spot on the coast. Biddeford's coastal community, called Biddeford Pool, has its own low-key place for seafood, Goldthwaite's (207-284-5000; poollobster.com; 3 Lester B. Orcutt Blvd.,

Goldthwaite's, Biddeford Pool

Nancy English

Biddeford Pool), where you order a lobster roll or something else at the counter, wait to be called, and enjoy your food at a picnic table in back near the water.

North of Saco's village on the commercial stretch of Rt. 1 an almost endless series of car sales lots is interrupted by a couple of amusement parks that have drawn local kids for decades. Funtown Splashtown USA (207-284-5139; funtown splashtownusa.com; 774 Portland Rd., Rt. 1, Saco)—you can get a pass if it rains and return along with the sun—has waterslides, kiddy rides, and a wooden roller coaster called Excalibur, built in 1998 (you must be 48 inches or taller to ride). The water park has a family raft slide among its many waterslides.

Aquaboggan Water Park (207-282-3112; aquabogganwaterpark.com; 980 Portland Rd., Rt. 1, Saco) has really fast, really high, really steep waterslides that your kids will haul you up and down on for hours. Little ones will never be interested in leaving the wave pool. Lure them away to the mini golf course to dry out.

A visit to Old Orchard Beach puts many attractions within walking distance—if you don't mind considering the ocean the best water park of all. Palace Playland (207-934-2001; palaceplayland.com; Rt. 1, Old Orchard Beach) is the town's amusement park, with a ferris wheel lighting the night sky and fireworks every Thursday night by the Pier. From the carousel for little people to Power Surge, for those 50 inches and taller, flinging your limbs in every direction, the rides are the attraction.

The Pier (oobpier.com) is its own world. First built in 1898, with concerts, a casino, and dancing, the tall structure stretched out over the waves until it was damaged by a storm. Repaired, it hosted crowds till a fire burned the entrance in 1907. Another storm chewed it up in 1909—and the repairs this time made the thing shorter. Frank Sinatra came to sing in the mid-1900s, the heyday. But in 1978 it seemed the thing was gone for good after a blizzard. Tradition proved too strong, however—it reopened in 1980. The Pier french fries are supposed to be terrific, and five restaurants and a variety of entertainment keep it hopping through the warm weather.

Motels line the main street. Those known to us as reliable include Billowhouse (207-934-2333; billowhouse.com; 2 Temple Ave., Ocean Park) and The Nautilus by the Sea (207-934-2021; nautilusbythesea.com; 2 Colby Ave., Ocean Park), both on the wide flat sandy beach that stretches for miles. Families will enjoy the sand south of Old Orchard Beach at Ocean Park, a 7-mile-long beach beside a summer community with a long history of camp meetings and Sunday-morning services. A music program and tennis courts are more aspects of Ocean Park's offerings.

Dinner in Old Orchard Beach can be readily enjoyed at The Landmark (207-934-0156; landmarkfinedining.com; 28 East Grand St., Old Orchard Beach), a local institution that keeps getting better. More elegant, though not at all formal, and equally historic, Joseph's by the Sea (207-934-5044; josephsbythesea.com; 55 W. Grand Ave., Old Orchard Beach) makes a dish called Pasta Maison, with angel-hair pasta, Maine shrimp, scallops, salmon, and mussels with cream that was a fine surprise—light and fresh and delicate.

Following Rt. 9 north past Pine Point—part of the town of Scarborough—will bring you to Ken's Place (207-883-6611; 207 Pine Point Rd., Rt. 9, Scarborough), where the fried clams are terrific and the first Tuesday of the month you can count on fried oysters.

Scarborough Marsh   Nancy English

Along that same stretch of road is the Scarborough Marsh Audubon Center, open seasonally (207-883-5100 May–Sept., for year-round information call 207-781-2330; maineaudubon.org; Pine Point Rd., Rt. 9, Scarborough). Linda Woodard runs the center, offering self-guided walks and canoe tours—you can rent canoes here—as well as guided tours like a full-moon tour of the marsh or an edible and medicinal plant walk. The birding is extraordinary.

Winslow Homer Studio, Scarborough
Nancy English

Another point of land in Scarborough rewards a visit. Black Point Rd. stretches out into the sea on a point of land that ends at Prouts Neck. This gated community holds the Winslow Homer Studio, now owned by Portland Museum of Art (see the Portland section that follows), though the museum does not plan to open the studio to the public till 2012, a schedule that has been repeatedly delayed. The museum holds events there, however. Although the studio is not open to the public, you can walk around it, if you walk to it from the Black Point Inn (207-883-2500; blackpointinn.com; 10 Black

Black Point Inn, Scarborough   Nancy English

Point Rd.). The inn deserves a visit in its own right, since under new management it has been serving really good food since 2009. It's a gracious old hostelry that has revamped and refocused on food and comfort. The 25 rooms are all top of the line in luxuriousness. This is reflected in the high prices, but remember that rates include a full breakfast and dinner, both likely to be worth your while. Golfing, tennis, beaches, and bikes are all at your disposal.

Another luxurious and tempting oceanfront inn sits on Rt. 77 in Cape Elizabeth is The Inn by the Sea (207-799-3134; innbythesea.com; 40 Bowery Beach Rd., Cape Elizabeth). Fifty-seven guest rooms range from enormous suites and two-bedroom cottages, all with a water view, to guest rooms with a gas fireplace. A pool, a spa, and a boardwalk to Crescent Beach State Park keep you entertained right where you are, and pet lovers love it here because they can bring their dogs, who come in for some high-end petting of their own. Sea Glass Restaurant is the inn's fine-dining restaurant, lately getting high praise.

Higgins Beach Inn (207-883-6684; higginsbeachinn.com; 34 Ocean Ave., Scarborough) is located in between those two high-end places, and its charming simple rooms are attractive and affordable, especially if they share a bath. The inn's good restaurant, Garofalo's, features really delicious Italian dishes and many recipes from innkeeper Diane Garofalo's family. Higgins Beach is a short block down the quiet street, and surfers like it for its good waves. Families love the flat, wide sandy beach, too, and the surfers are kept off to the sides of the beach during prime beach hours.

Finally, but with the highest scenic importance, a visit to Portland Head Light in Fort Williams Park cannot be beat. The park holds decaying Goddard Mansion and Fort Williams, busiest during World War II, but Maine's oldest lighthouse, Portland Head Light (207-799-2661; portlandheadlight.com; 1000 Shore Rd., Cape Elizabeth) with its own museum in the keeper's quarters, is the main attraction. The lighthouse first warned mariners in 1791. It's a perfect setting for a picnic and for flying kites, while the rolling grassy hills and short oceanside path are other diversions.

Portland

Check out these great attractions and activities . . .

Walkable Portland holds several museums within a few blocks, starting with the biggest, the Portland Museum of Art (207-775-6148; portlandmuseum .org; 7 Congress Square). It's open daily, 10–5 Memorial through Columbus Days, Fridays until 9, closed Mon. off-season; closed major holidays. The modern building that holds most of the exhibits was designed by Henry N. Cobb of

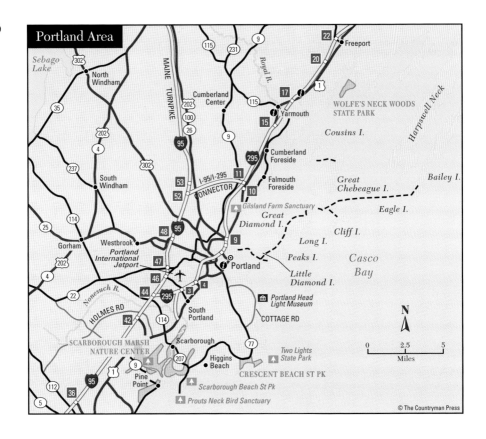

I. M. Pei & Partners and built in 1983. Among its pleasures is the view from the inside out, across Congress Square. If you can turn away from the windows, the walls will reward you with art by Winslow Homer, Edward Hopper, Andrew Wyeth, some examples of the works of Picasso and Matisse, and many more. The 1801 McLellan House, where the museum was first opened, is a Federal mansion restored to its glory with frenetic wallpapers and carpets—the bold patterns and colors dismayed some visitors at first. In between is the L. D. M. Sweat Memorial Galleries, built in 1911 by John Calvin Stevens, which hold some of the museum's most loved 19th-century paintings and sculptures. Painter John Marin will be the subject of a 2011 summer exhibition, with his modernist abstract paintings and sketches of the ocean at Cape Split, in Down East Maine, the focus.

The Children's Museum of Maine (207-828-1234; kitetails.org; 142 Free St.) is next door, a perfect spot to let the kids get rid of their energy after a tour of artwork, in the model lobster boat or the fire engine, the grocery store or the ATM.

Down Congress St. a few blocks toward the sea is the Maine Historical Society (207-774-1822; mainehistory.org; 485 Congress St.), with a newly renovated library. Work on the library knocked out a lot of the old plantings in the lovely garden, but the Longfellow Garden Society was not deterred, and the peaceful oasis in middle of the Portland is recovering nicely—it's open to the public. Just walk past the buildings and you'll find it. There are period furnishings in the

Wadsworth-Longfellow House, built in 1785 by the grandfather of Henry Wadsworth Longfellow, the poet who was born in Portland and whose statue stands in Longfellow Square; tours are offered most days. The Maine Historical Society Museum holds changing exhibits.

Across the street on Brown St. is the Museum of African Culture (207-871-7188; museumofafricanculture.org; 13 Brown St.), the creation of founder Oscar Mokeme, a descendant of Nigerian Igbo royal family healers. His collection of masks, bronzes, batiks, and wooden sculptures comes to life when he dons one for a ceremonial blessing.

Victoria Mansion (207-772-4841; victoriamansion.org; 109 Danforth St.) is a pleasant walk down Park St. past some of Portland's prettiest town houses. The mansion was built in 1858 by Ruggles Sylvester Morse, who made a fortune with New Orleans hotels; this was to be his summer home. The mansion was scheduled to be demolished in 1940 but was saved by a retired teacher, William Holmes, who used his own money. Room interiors created by Gustave Herter and 90 percent of the original furnishings make this mansion, the finest surviving Italian-villa-style house in America, remarkable. Its holiday decorations take the elaboration even higher. Don't miss the Turkish Smoking Room.

Greater Portland Landmarks Center for Architecture and Preservation (207-774-5561; portlandlandmarks.org; 93 High St.) is just down Danforth and up High, and its library is a fund of information about architecture in Portland. The center provides a variety of tours of Portland, including Homes of Portland's Golden Age, 1800–1860, which shows off the city's Federal, Greek Revival, and Italianate houses. The Portland Observatory gets its own tour. This maritime signal tower on the top of Munjoy Hill, a long walk across town, gives visitors who climb up its stairs a great view of Casco Bay and the White Mountains.

Portland Trails (207-775-2411; trails.org; 305 Commercial St.) has developed more than 30 miles of trails in and around Portland—the trail map is sold on the website. But from Casco Bay Lines on Commercial St. a wide paved path makes a great hike around Eastern Promenade, and intrepid walkers will be able to cirle the entire peninsula to reach Baxter Blvd., a charming path filled with Portlanders in search of exercise every lovely day of the year.

Narrated tours can be enjoyed with Mainely Tours and Gifts (207-774-0808; mainelytours.com; 3 Moulton St.) and Downeast Duck Tours (207-774-3825; downeastduck.com; 177 Commercial St.). Spirits Alive (207-846-7753; spiritsalive.org) is a group dedicated to protecting the Eastern Cemetery (gates at 224 Congress St.), and it guides visits to the graves through the summer on Sunday afternoons, describing the lives of the

Portland's Middle St.   Nancy English

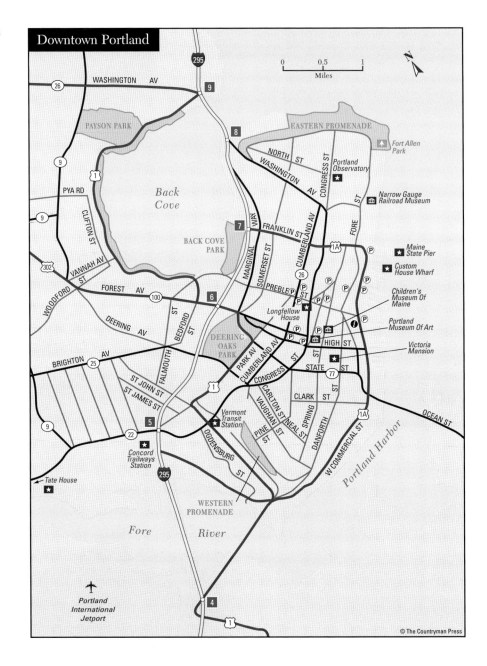

Downtown Portland

people buried here. Around Halloween, you might encounter the ghosts of those folks themselves—or perhaps they're actors—during the Walk Among the Shadows, a benefit for the organization held in early evening.

Maine Foodie Tours (800-979-3370; mainefoodietours.com) travel on foot or on a trolley to fish stores, cheese shops, bakeries, and breweries, providing samples to keep you hungry for more.

Checking In

Best places to stay in Portland

Foodie Tours, Portland   Nancy English

You visited the museums, took the tours—now where are you going to stay? The West End, Portland's wealthiest neighborhood, holds a few fine bed & breakfasts. The Morrill Mansion Bed & Breakfast (207-774-6900; morrillmansion.com; 249 Vaughan St.) has seven comfortably furnished rooms, each with private bath, with a feeling of luxury and fairly reasonable rates. Full breakfasts and afternoon treats keep guests happy, as they do at The Chadwick (207-774-2137; the chadwick.com; 140 Chadwick St.), with its back garden.

Fancier rooms at The Pomegranate Inn (207-772-1006; pomegranate inn.com; 49 Neal St.) are decorated in a bold, colorful style by Heidi Gerquest, a Portland artist, but off-season rates are available. The Danforth (207-879-6557; danforthmaine.com; 164 Danforth St.) is in an elegant building with refurbished rooms. Like the Pomegranate Inn, this inn was purchased by Kim Swan and updated.

The Wild Iris (207-775-0224; wildirisinn.com; 273 State St.) is comfortable and casual, and rooms with shared bath are reasonably priced. It's also close to downtown, though the first part of your walk is uphill. A little farther away, The Inn at St. John (207-773-6481; innatstjohn.com; 939 Congress St.) is a favorite of budget-conscious travelers.

People who prefer hotels with up-to-date amenities and the pleasure of breakfasting alone and unmolested can find a room at the Portland Regency (207-774-4200; theregency.com; 20 Milk St.), with its own health club and a good bar called The Armory Lounge. But the fact that the building was once an armory has made the layout of some of the rooms a little odd—the windows are high, and there is no view. Guests in Hilton Garden Inn (207-780-0780; hiltongardeninnport land.com; 65 Commercial St.) can see across the street into the ferry dock and enjoy an indoor pool. Portland Harbor Hotel (207-775-9090; theport landharborhotel.com; 468 Fore St.) has rooms that might offer marble bathrooms, glassed-in showers, granite counters, and an oval spa tub.

Local Flavors

The taste of Portland—local restaurants, cafés, and more

Dinner

Remarkably, after several years of new restaurant openings, almost all of Portland's dining spots are sustaining themselves with enthusiastic crowds. It's been clear to the restaurateurs who cruise the streets and peer into the restaurant storefronts, wondering what the economic recession has done to dining out, that Portland has become a town that invests heavily in dinner.

Customers do even better for themselves, with a variety of cuisines from Ethiopian and Cajun to haute French and down-home Down East. Visitors who plan their day around meals have some work to do to narrow down the choices, but this will make it easier for you. We've divided the spectrum into expensive, reasonable, and cheap, which does not in the least speak to which is best. In fact, there is no easy answer to the question *Which is your favorite restaurant*, because there are so many places to love for so many different reasons.

It's easy enough to start at the top of the heap with Hugo's (207-774-8538; hugos.net; 88 Middle St., Portland), an elegant restaurant that serves dishes that combine fabulous flavor and beautiful looks. "It's aggressive food," said chef and part-owner Rob Evans—a James Beard Award winner—on a short video on his website. But like the pork belly no one had heard of when he and his partner Nancy Pugh opened in 2000, inventive and novel ingredients are pleasures many diners now adore. Pan-fried lamb's tongue with lentil salad, from the bar menu for $15, appeared in 2010 with grilled beef heart Caesar.

Back Bay Grill (207-772-8833; backbaygrill.com; 65 Portland St.) rewards every visitor, whether you order a martini at the bar or go for a dish from every course on the menu. Hudson Valley foie gras with pickled bing cherries; the best crabcake in the state; the signature organic Scottish salmon, perhaps with chanterelles—all are brilliant proof this is the place you want to dine.

Fore Street (207-775-2717; fore-street.biz; 288 Fore St., Portland) opened in June 1996, bringing chef and part-owner Sam Hayward's obsession with local fresh ingredients into action amid a big, somewhat rustic, and often busy and noisy space. Almond butter on the wood-oven-roasted mussels makes them addictive, and spit-roasted pork loin and seared hanger steak have their own fan club. Best of all are seasonal items like summer lamb, fall squash, and winter scallops. Hayward was awarded the Best Chef Northeast medal from the James Beard Foundation in 2004.

Miyake (207-871-9170; restaurant miyake.com; 129 Spring St.; BYOB) serves the best sushi in town, but that's an understatement. Try the omakase, or chef's choice, because owner-chef Masa Miyake has a sure sense of flavors and puts together make and sushi that will delight your taste buds: a touch of heat, the richness of a quail egg, perhaps silky wild salmon, and so many other things. If you're in luck, one of them will be fresh uni. Pai Men Miyake (207-541-9204; 188 State St.) is a sister restaurant devoted to noodles and broths like elixirs, popular from the moment the doors opened.

Bar Lola (207-775-5652; barlola .net; 100 Congress St.) is up Munjoy Hill, serving a very reasonable five-course prix fixe ($39 in 2010) that will take you from pork belly confit with duck liver mousse, to smoked duck breast, to carrot salad with white-port-soaked apricots, to steak with smoked corn pudding. How about ending with roasted banana crêpe?

Bresca (207-772-1004; restaurant bresca.com; 111 Middle St.) holds 20 or so seats, and they're usually filled. Make reservations and look forward to wondering how chorizo-and-Gorgonzola-stuffed dates can be quite so good, or why so many Portlanders insist on always ordering the shaved brussels sprouts with toasted walnuts and Parmesan. Braised kale with a six-minute egg, pancetta, and kombu butter is another conundrum, seemingly simple and ridiculously exciting. Do not omit dessert. Chef-owner Krista Desjarlais, a former pastry chef, puts together masterpieces; one of her classics is the buttermilk panna cotta.

Caiola's (207-772-1110; caiolas .com; 58 Pine St.) is many people's favorite restaurant, relaxing, welcoming, and fun, with Abby Harmon's sure touch in the kitchen assuring that dinner will be wonderful. In late fall it might start with lobster pudding with corn salad—and in early spring there might be a ramp custard that we've never forgotten. The burger is great, and so are the grilled hanger steak, paella, and grilled daurade.

Emilitsa (207-221-0245; emilitsa .com; 547 Congress St.) serves the owner's mother's Greek food, plates of lamb chops, a beautiful whole roast fish, and starters of tangy and richly flavored spreads. The bread will be crusty, the feta creamy and sharp, the wine acidic and strong; the vegetables are prepared with olive oil, lemon, garlic, and herbs in ways you will wish you could emulate every night at home.

Cinque Terre (207-347-6154; cinqueterremaine.com; 36 Wharf St.) is the more formal, more elegant side and Vignola (207-772-1330; vignola maine.com; 10 Dana St.) the rowdier, noisier spot serving thin-crust pizza, but both have fine Italian wine lists and a knack for Italian cured meats, zesty salads, and pasta tender and fresh, wrapped around lobster in ravioli or covered with house pancetta ragu. The gnocchi is fantastic, and much of what's

on the plate comes from the owners' farm.

five fifty-five (207-761-0555; five fifty-five.com; 55 Congress St.) has a comfortable bar area and a bar menu for a quick introduction to Steve Corry's fine cooking. Hanger steak with a tomato and blue cheese tartlet, seared yellowfin tuna with an egg, kalamata tapenade and potato salad, or seared monkfish with succotash and lemon-thyme lobster broth could make an evening out special indeed. The kitchen comes up with some spectacular ice creams worth sampling, and this is a great place for brunch.

Brunch is also fine at Local 188 (207-761-7909; local188.com; 685 Congress St.), a good place to meet for drinks that comes up with good specials and small plates, too. House gnocchi, seared shrimp, and chorizo in Romesco sauce with penne and a house paella are specialties. Tapas ranging $4–14 would make perfect snacks for a light appetite.

Sonny's (207-772-7774; sonnys portland.com; 83 Exchange St.) is owned by the same folks as Local 188. The historic space, a former bank, is remarkably attractive, and the bar area sleek and modern. Seviche, mussels in sweet lime coconut broth, and salt fish stamp & go capture the Caribbean inflection of the menu. Cuban skirt steak and mariscada, a daily spicy seafood stew, can be wonderful.

Moderately priced, the Grill Room (207-774-2333; hardinglee smith.com; 84 Exchange St.) is one of three restaurants owned by Harding Lee Smith, who started his own entrepreneurial career after years of cooking for others on Munjoy Hill with his successful Front Room (207-773-3366; 73 Congress St.), with comfort food, generous portions, and lots of butter and salt. At the Grill Room, grilled steaks and fish are the center of the steak-house menu, but he keeps the prices low somehow or other, even when the chicken is organic.

The Corner Room (207-879-4747; 110 Exchange St.) is one block up the street from the Grill Room, but its menu centers on Italian specialties, and the fresh house pasta does a lot of the work of making dishes stand out. We haven't tried the pizza because we like the pappardelle with wild mushrooms and cream too much. Cocktails at the small bar were developed and refined or recovered from the dust of history by John Myers, a bartender who knows the history of the cocktail from ingredients to techniques.

Paciarino (207-774-3500; paciarino.com; 468 Fore St.) serves its own excellent fresh pasta in classic dishes you really cannot hope to taste except in Italy, or at least that's how it used to be. House goat cheese ravioli with caramelized onion, or seafood ravioli with sweet Maine shrimp, can be bought to cook at home as well as enjoyed in the restaurant.

Inexpensive Dining

Nosh Kitchen Bar (207-553-2227; 551 Congress St.) gets better and better. Spicy tuna confit salad with toasted almonds on greens dressed with a sesame vinaigrette made a lunch to remember, and the folks who tried the burger and crunchy fries—with bacon dust!—enjoyed themselves just as much. Late nights and lunches along with dinner hours keep the door open, as do plates of house-cured meat and an exceptional beer list.

Otto and Enzo (207-773-7099; ottoportland.com; 576 Congress St.) prove that cheap food can provide as exalted an experience as it is expensive. Pizza by the slice, thin crust and marvelous, is sold on the left in Otto, to be eaten at a stool in the tiny customer area, on the sidewalk at a seat in good weather, or on your walk home. The mashed potato, scallion, and bacon is perfection, and the mushroom and cauliflower does just as well. Next door you can sit at a table and eat the great pizza, order a whole pie and share it, and drink some inexpensive plonk or beer and have a salad. No dessert, no other things on the menu. No one minds.

Boda (207-347-7557; bodamaine.com; 671 Congress St.) serves Thai street food, and again a taste of what the real stuff is like makes you wish all the Thai places in town would attempt to be equally authentic. Pummelo fruit salad on betel leaves, with coconut, peanut, lime, ginger, and shrimp, is an example, and the beef Thai curry is far beefier and less sweet than you might be used to.

Bonobo (207-347-8267; bonobopizza.com; 46 Pine St.) has excellent pizza, cooked in a wood-fired oven, and the namesake version with mushrooms, prosciutto, spinach, leeks, Fontina, and cream can't be beat. Good wine, several salads, and soups round out the menu.

Flatbread Company (207-772-8777; flatbreadcompany.com; 72 Commercial St.) is a chain of high-quality, wood-fired pizza places, and Portland's is right on the water. Enjoy your flatbread overlooking Casco Bay Lines, and order from the outdoor window.

Duck Fat (207-774-8080; duckfat.com; 43 Middle St.) is owned by Rob Evans and Nancy Pugh of Hugo's. Their vision for a lunch place with crisp panini, extraordinary fries cooked up with duck fat, soup, salad, and specials, has kept folks coming back. The milk shakes will intoxicate you with their richness; the Original is made with double Tahitian vanilla bean crème anglaise gelato.

Order outside at the Flatbread Company, Portland   *Nancy English*

14 Veranda St.) with pho and vermicelli dishes, are fine examples of conventional Thai restaurants.

Asmara (207-253-5122; 51 Oak St.) should not be missed. This Eritrean restaurant is run by Asmeret Teklu, who makes fresh injera, a soft, delicious bread you use to scoop up the cooked greens, meat, and beans. Springy and resilient, the ancient bread has a refreshing sour flavor that makes a fine contrast with the long-cooked, savory dishes—perhaps collards or red lentils, or lamb stew with okra—served for both lunch and dinner.

Oh No Café (207-774-0773; ohnocafe.com; 87 Brackett St.) is a neighborhood place you'll want to drive to for a fantastic sandwich, fine soups, and wonderful breakfast specials. The roast chicken with avocado, tomato, and red onion is one favorite, but we always go for the grilled hanger steak salad with cucumbers and blue cheese.

158 Picket Street Café (207-799-8998; 158 Benjamin Pickett St., South Portland) makes soups with heat and depth, and sandwiches that resound with pesto and fresh mozzarella or chutney and cured meat. The egg on a bagel with cheese and ham makes breakfast irresistible, and the house-cured salmon is pretty wonderful on those chewy fresh bagels, too.

Happy Teriyaki (207-771-2000; 630 Congress St.) makes a spicy tofu stew that will heat you up on the coldest day of winter, when the sizzling beef dishes and spicy kimchee would make it possible to shoulder the cold with aplomb.

Veranda Thai Cuisine (207-874-0045; verandathaicuisine.com; 9 Veranda St.) and its sibling business across the street, Veranda Noodle Bar (207-874-9090; verandanoodlebar.com;

Prepared Food and Bakeries
Standard Baking Company sells bread from the bakery downstairs (207-773-2112; 75 Commercial St., Portland), a resource for scones and luscious morning buns). The business shares ownership with Fore Street. Beware the dessert menu's peach tarte tatin.

Portland Shopping

The shopping around Exchange St. features fine clothing stores worth checking out, but more curious and surprising finds lie east on Congress St. on the other side of Franklin Arterial. **Angela Adams** at 273 Congress St. sells purses and bags with the bold graphic prints that have made her rugs famous. Just up the street, **Ferdinand** at 243 Congress St. has a signature squirrel at the drums on T-shirts and baby's bibs. Walk down India St., take a right on Middle St., and find **Rabelais** (207-774-1044; rabelaisbooks.com; 86 Middle St.), the world's best cooking- and food-obsessed bookstore.

Standard Baking Company, Portland

Nancy English

Rosemont Markets (207-774-8129 at 580 Brighton Ave., and 207-773-7888 at 88 Congress St., Portland;

At the Portland Farmers' Markets

Nancy English

rosemontmarket.com) makes wonderful pies with seasonal fruit, cakes and quiche, meat loaf, and its own pastrami, sandwiches, soups, spreads, and sauces. It also stocks local vegetables, fruits, and berries, fine cheeses from Maine and far afield, good-priced wines, and provisions of all kinds.

Scratch Baking Company (207-799-0668; scratchbakingco.com; 416 Preble St.) is worth a trip to South Portland to taste the slow rise, chewy levain, country white, and sour rye. Bagels are a specialty, and the pastries exceptional.

Aurora Provisions (207-871-9060; auroraprovisions; 64 Pine St.) makes a fine dinner; the dolmathes among its prepared foods and lemon bars among the delectable baked goods are both excellent examples. You can get everything you need here, from soup to nuts, wine to coffee.

Arabica in Portland   Nancy English

Speaking of coffee, Arabica (207-899-1833; 2 Free St.) roasts its own beans and sells them, as well as brewing them for fine cappuccinos, lattes, and espressos in their airy coffeehouse. Crisp, fresh toast with butter is a specialty, unusually fine because of the chewy fresh bread they stock from a local baker. Bard Coffee (207-899-4788; bardcoffee.net; 185 Middle St.) has a fine location and even better cup of coffee. Of course there is free WiFi.

The Portland Farmers Markets, on Saturday morning in Deering Oaks Park and on Wednesday through the lunch hour at Monument Square, attract crowds who come to gaze in adoration at the result of farmers' months-long labors. The produce gets better and better, and surely someone is eating her vegetables, because so many of us are buying them.

Peaks Island and Chebeague Island

Attractions, activities, accommodations, eateries, etc.

Casco Bay Lines (207-774-7871; cascobaylines.com; 56 Commercial St., Portland) is the starting point for an excursion out to the islands of Casco Bay. Its red-and-yellow ferries make several trips daily year-round to commuter-filled Peaks Island, where a meal and a walk or a bicycle ride comprise an excellent day trip. Down Front is the name of the part of the island near the ferry dock, reached after a mere 20 minutes on the ferry, and it's also the location of the island's store, post office, two inns, and a few restaurants.

The Inn on Peaks Island (207-766-5100; innonpeaks.com; 33 Island Ave., Peaks Island) sits at the top of the little hill you climb after getting off the ferry. Its handsome rooms provide excellent retreats, with cottage furniture and views, while the dining room with outdoor seating in good weather makes terrific fried clams, fried Maine shrimp, and burgers as well as more serious entrées like BBQ blueberry-glazed pork chops and prime rib on Friday and Saturday nights. In 2010 a room and dinner for two was $185.

Cockeyed Gull (207-766-2800; cockeyedgull.com; 78 Island Ave., Peaks Island) is an institution on the island with a twist—the Korean owner, whose grilled salmon and rack of lamb are second to none out here, can also make some fine Korean dishes. The deck has an incredible view of Portland's harbor glimmering in the distance, and the sunset.

Brad's Bikes (207-766-5631; 115 Island Ave., Peaks Island) rents bikes, often on the honor system, with a box to put your money in and a selection of

Casco Bay Lines

Nancy English

well-maintained bikes to choose from. A bike trip around the island takes a leisure-ly 45 minutes, but a few stops and explorations of the rocky coves fill the day up quickly. When you park your bike back at Brad's and head to the ferry, there's always time for an ice cream cone at Down Front, at the top of the hill by the ferry dock.

Chebeague Island is an hour and a half away from Portland, when you ride the ferry from Casco Bay Lines. Anyone interested in staying awhile will prefer to park at the Rt. 1, Yarmouth, parking lot of Chebeague Transportation Company (207-846-3700; chebeaguetrans.com; Chebeague Island). After you pay a parking fee you climb into a bus for a ride (included in the parking charge) to the dock on Cousins Island, where the ferry picks up passengers to Chebeague. The Chebeague Island Inn (207-846-5155; chebeagueislandinn.com; 61 South Rd., Chebeague Island) was under new ownership in 2010 and proved its hospitality during one evening's visit. The upscale menu makes dinner an event, most of it completely satisfying. The long, wide porch filled with wicker chairs will always be a lovely place to take in the sunset and enjoy a drink at the end of a day exploring the island, and the golf course between that porch and the water is open to visi-tors. Your island explorations will also be assisted by the generosity of Mac Pas-sano, the Bike Man of Chebeague, who provides bicycles for free.

Freeport and Yarmouth

Attractions, activities, accommodations, eateries, etc.

L.L. Bean (877-755-2326; llbean.com; 95 Main St., Freeport) is open, as many of you know, 24 hours a day, 365 days of the year. That's lucky for the warehouse workers on the third shift who want to go Christmas shopping at 3 AM when work lets out (the warehouses that fulfill phone orders are down Desert Rd.) and just as lucky for the tourists driving through Freeport anytime of the day or night. Believe us, the buildings are peaceful and quiet late at night. Although the round-the-clock hours pertain only to the Flagship Store, the L.L. Bean Hunting & Fishing Store, the L.L. Bean Bike, Boat & Ski Store, the L.L. Bean Home Store, and the L.L. Bean Outlet are certainly open late into the night as the Christmas holidays approach. The L.L. Bean complex is decked out with its own tall holiday tree flashing light, and the town does it right, too.

Sparkle Weekend (freeportusa.com has the full event listing) in Freeport includes tree lighting next to L.L. Bean, carolers, free hot cocoa, and free horse-drawn carriage rides every afternoon and into the early evening on Saturday and Sunday from late November to late December.

In almost any weather the company hosts Walk-On Adventures, in which anyone can enjoy an introduction to a variety of sports by paying $20 and calling 877-755-2326 or signing up at the Outdoor Discovery School kiosk in the Flagship Store. Scenic kayak tours, a four-hour trip, are sometimes offered just for women and cost $59 in 2010. Target skills and target clays are other possibilities—all equipment is provided.

In 2010 there were more than 60 shops to check out in Freeport. Coffee shops like Isabella's Sticky Buns (207-865-6635; 2 School St., just off Rt. 1 one block north of L.L. Bean) provides the necessary coffee and cinnamon bun to get you through the day, as well as terrific sandwiches and soup. A customer who really wishes to unwind will find all exquisite at Jacqueline's Tea Room (207-865-2123; 201 Main St.), by reservation only 11 AM–3 PM, where tea is a ceremony and the busy world is worlds away.

But maybe you don't think about eating as soon as the subject of shopping comes up, like us. In that case, consider the intersection of Bow and Main streets in Freeport the center of your world. On the western side of the street are all the L.L. Bean stores except the Outlet, which is now located in the newly built Freeport Village Station (207-552-7772; onefreeportvillagestation.com), just a few steps down Bow St. and to your right. Also in Freeport Village Station are outlets for Nike, Calvin Klein, Coach, Brooks Brothers, and Famous Footwear. Parking lots are located just off Main St. on both sides, including inside the parking garage of Freeport Village Station (enter from Depot or Mill St.).

Along Main St. you'll see Burberry, Cole Haan, Jones New York, and Polo Ralph Lauren. Down Bow St. look for J. Crew and The North Face.

Thos. Moser Cabinetmakers (207-865-4519; thosmoser.com; 149 Main St.) is at the north end of the village, and shows off wooden handcrafted furniture with lines as graceful as a the flight of a migrating seabird.

Cold River Vodka (207-865-4828; coldrivervodka.com; 437 Rt. 1) is south of the village on a stretch of Rt. 1 worth driving to, not only to tour the distillery of

Harraseeket Lunch & Lobster, South Freeport   Nancy English

this award-winning business—one of the first of Maine's boutique distilleries—but also to visit Cuddledown's Outlet (207-865-1713; cuddledown.com; 554 Rt. 1) and discover your own best deal among the many storefronts in this busy section of the coast.

For both shopping and dining, Harraseeket Inn (207-865-9377; harraseeket inn.com; 162 Main St.) cannot be beat. The elegant inn has an indoor pool, a formal and exceptional fine-dining restaurant, The Maine Dining Room, and a more casual but very good breakfast, lunch, and dinner place called The Broad Arrow Tavern. Both emphasize local and wild food sources, and The Broad Arrow is decorated like a Maine camp.

If you wish to decorate your home that way, The Mangy Moose (207-865-6414; themangymoose.com; 112 Main St.) has everything you need, from moose antlers to a taxidermied bobcat—but more typical of this fun store are the Maine embroidered pillows, great books, and maple syrup.

Brewster House Bed & Breakfast (207-865-4121; brewsterhouse.com; 180 Main St.), James Place Inn (207-865-4486; jamesplaceinn.com; 11 Holbrook St.), and White Cedar Inn (207-865-9099; whitecedarinn.com; 178 Main St.) are all well-run B&Bs, serving good breakfasts to their guests and providing the personal touch and local knowledge so helpful to visitors.

At any of those inns, you're likely to hear a recommendation for the Mediterranean Grill (207-865-1688; mediterraneangrill.biz; 10 School St.), which makes good kebabs, spanakopita, and moussaka. Of course, you might not have yet satisfied your taste for lobster, and a scenic spot to crack open a freshly steamed lobster is close at hand: Harraseeket Lunch & Lobster (207-865-4888; harraseeketlunch andlobster.com; Main St., South Freeport). Order lobster and steamers at one window in the back, on a deck overlooking the water, and fried seafood at another by the picnic tables and awning.

Brunswick and the Harpswells

INCLUDING BATH AND THE PHIPPSBURG/GEORGETOWN PENINSULAS

Coastal Rt. 1 offers easy access but no views of Brunswick, Maine's premier college town, or of Bath, the handsome old shipbuilding city that's home to the Maine Maritime Museum. The highway double-barrels past both communities, short-changing them along with the Midcoast's most convenient, yet surprisingly peaceful peninsulas and bridge-linked islands.

Between its Brunswick and Bath exits, Rt. 1 shadows the Androscoggin River for a way, giving motorists a glimpse of the area's many hundreds of miles of waterfront. Two of Maine's longest and mightiest rivers—the Kennebec and the Androscoggin—meet in Merrymeeting Bay above Bath. Cove-notched peninsulas stretch south from both communities.

Harpswell, south of Brunswick, is known for its seafood restaurants but also offers some of the coast's best kayaking. Phippsburg and Georgetown, south of Bath, are home to the Midcoast's biggest and best beaches.

Brunswick

Check out these great attractions and activities . . .

If you want to continue along the coast, you have to leave I-295 and switch to Rt. 1 at Brunswick (brunswickdown town.org). Exit 28 puts you abruptly on a commercial strip; at a particularly long light, Rt. 1 angles off to the left. Continue straight instead, up leafy Pleasant St. to Maine St. Turn right and look for the Brunswick Visitors Center (restrooms) in Brunswick Station. This new complex anticipates the 2012 arrival of Amtrak's Downeaster (thedowneaster.com) from Boston and offers ample free parking. It's also the departure point for the Maine Eastern Railroad (see the sidebar). Park here and stroll, either up Maine St. to the Bowdoin College (bowdoin.edu) campus, or down to shops and restaurants.

Brunswick's Maine St. is the widest main street in the state, laid out in 1717 with a grassy "mall" near the upper end, the scene of farmer's markets and summer band concerts. Its long lower blocks are lined with shops, galleries, and

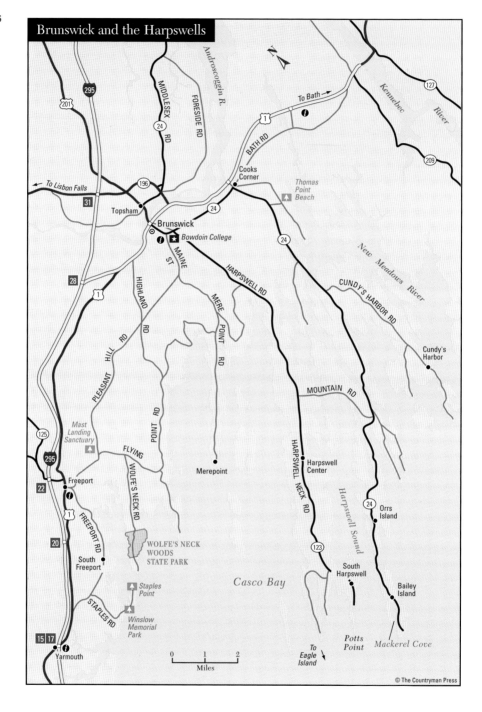

Brunswick and the Harpswells

© The Countryman Press

Brunswick Farmers' Market on the Mall   Christina Tree

restaurants. This is a true college town with reasonably priced restaurants, an outstanding bookstore (Gulf of Maine Books, 134 Maine St.), and frequent alternative films at Eveningstar Cinema (149 Maine St.) and the Frontier Café & Cinema Gallery (14 Maine St.). Galleries cluster at the lower end of the street. Second Friday Art Walks (fiveriverartsalliance.org) reveal many more studios and other art venues along the way.

The Pickard Theater at Bowdoin College

Christina Tree

Founded in 1794, Bowdoin is not only the pride of but also very much a part of Brunswick. Its visitor-friendly campus is the July and August venue for the Bowdoin International Music Festival (bowdoinfestival.org) and for the Maine State Music Theater (msmt.org), Maine's most popular summer stage. The nearby Bowdoin College Museum of Art (bowdoin.edu/artmuseum) has been recently renovated and expanded, the better to

Joshua Chamberlain

Local historians argue that the Civil War began and ended in Brunswick—and a case can be made. It was here that Harriet Beecher Stowe penned *Uncle Tom's Cabin*, a book credited with starting the war; and Joshua Chamberlain—the Bowdoin College professor (and later president) considered Maine's greatest Civil War hero—was the Union general chosen to accept the South's surrender at Appomattox. Thanks to the Ken Burns PBS *Civil War* series and a spate of Civil War films and books, Chamberlain's popularity has surged in recent years. The **Joshua Chamberlain Home and Museum,** 226 Maine St., has been rescued from demolition and largely restored by the Pejepscot Historical Society (207-729-6606). Chamberlain (1828–1914) is best remembered for his valor and leadership defending Little Round Top during the Battle of Gettysburg. He ended the war as a major general and was chosen by General Grant to meet with General Robert E. Lee at Appomattox. As the Confederate regiments marched into the Union camp to lay down their arms, Chamberlain had his troops salute them, a gesture of respect that infuriated some Northerners but helped reconcile many Southerners to defeat. After the war Chamberlain served four one-year terms as governor of Maine, and served 1881–1883 as president of Bowdoin College. The house itself evokes the sense of this intriguing man—as well as of a young Henry Wordsworth Longfellow, who lived here in 1832–1833 while a student at Bowdoin, three decades before Chamberlain moved in.

Joshua Lawrence Chamberlain
Pejepscot Historical Society

display its varied collection and changing exhibits, which include contemporary artists. Don't miss the Peary-MacMillan Arctic Museum, hidden away in Hubbard Hall. It's a trove of trophy Arctic wildlife and gear from the pioneer attempts by Bowdoin graduates Robert Peary and Donald Baxter MacMillan to reach the North Pole. For more about the colorful and controversial Admiral Peary—and his role in the 1890s equivalent to the 1960s race to the moon—visit his ship-shaped home on Eagle Island

Poet Gary Lawless presides over the Gulf of Maine Bookstore in Brunswick.

Christina Tree

Eagle Island State Historical Site

Christina Tree

(pearyeagleisland.org), now a state historic site, accessible by the sailboat *Symbion II* (207-725-0969).

Tip: Brunswick's museums are closed Monday; seasonal farmer's markets on the Mall are held Tuesday and Friday.

Maine RR Excursion and Expansion

The Maine Eastern Railroad (866-637-2457; maineeasternrailroad.com) runs Fri. and Sat., Memorial Day weekend–late June, then Wed.–Sun. until early Nov. The

54-mile run from Brunswick to Rockland—with stops in Bath and Wiscasset—takes just over two hours, traveling along the coast in plush, streamlined 1940s and '50s coaches and dining car, pulled by a 1950s diesel electric engine. Check the website for current schedule and fares. The **Amtrak Downeaster** (thedowneaster.com) from Boston, which presently comes only as far as Portland, is due to reach Brunswick in 2012. Plans call for the Maine Eastern to expand its season and adjust its schedule to connect with the Downeaster. In the meantime Brunswick Station, opened in 2010, serves as the town's information center and departure point for the Maine Eastern.

Maine Eastern Railroad

Christina Tree

The Harpswells

Check out these great
attractions and activities . . .

Famed for its seafood restaurants, this town is a great place to stay. Generally known as "The Harpswells" because it's so ragged, cut by water and stitched by bridges, it claims hundreds of islands and more shoreline than any other town in Maine. Harpswell Sound is a particularly appealing, sheltered place for kayaking—and H_2Outfitters (h2outfitters.com), sited at the Cribstone Bridge on Orrs Island, is in a great spot to access it. They offer tours ranging from a few hours to several days.

From Maine St. at the edge of the Bowdoin campus, Rt. 123 runs south, past farm stands and gallery signs. In Harpswell Center the 1775 white-clapboard Elijah Kellogg Church, named for a former pastor who was a popular 19th-century children's book author, faces the matching Harpswell Town Meeting House across the road. Admittedly, most people who come this far are on their way to two of the area's popular seafood restaurants (see *Places to Eat*).

Most tourists actually turn off Rt. 123 six miles below Brunswick, onto Mountain Rd., which crosses Harpswell Sound on its way to Sebascodegan Island. The road ends at Rt. 24, where a right takes you through scenic Orrs Island and across the recently rebuilt Cribstone Bridge. Built with granite blocks, laid honeycomb-fashion to allow tidal flows, the bridge puts you on Bailey Island. Continue past picturesque Mackerel Cove and keep an eye out for Washington Ave. on the left. Park at the small shingled building here that's an Episcopal church and follow the

H2Outfitters on Orrs Island   Christina Tree

signs and path along the water to the Giant Staircase. The staircase itself is a series a clefts in the cliffs with a flight of smooth boulders rising through the surf. The rocks all along this path look deceptively soft, like petrified driftwood.

Back on Rt. 24 continue to Land's End, where a large gift store and small statue by Casco Bay honor Maine fishermen. Return up Rt. 24 to Rt. 1. There are plenty of photo and shopping ops along the way. Cundy's Harbor, a well-marked 7-mile roundtrip detour, is another place to savor seafood with a view of lobster and sailboats in another quiet inlet.

Checking In

Best places to stay in Brunswick and the Harpswells

Brunswick Inn (207-729-4914; brunswickbnb.com; 165 Park Row, Brunswick) is a gracious B&B in an 1800s Greek Revival mansion separated from at the upper end of Maine St. and its traffic by the grassy "mall," but within walking distance of both the Bowdoin College campus and downtown shops and restaurants. The 15 guest rooms are divided between the original house and a contemporary carriage house in the rear.

Harpswell Inn (207-853-5509; harpswellinn.com; 108 Lookout Point Rd., Harpswell) was once an annex to one of the 52 now-vanished hotels and boardinghouses in Harpswell during the steamboating era. With lawns sloping to the water near a quiet point, this three-story, white-clapboard B&B offers peace, all the comforts, and easy access to kayaking and lobster pounds. Middle Bay Farm Bed & Breakfast (207-373-1375; middlebayfarm.com; 287 Pennellville Rd., Brunswick), sited on a quiet cove, is a particularly beautiful spot. There are four guest rooms in the gracious 1830s main house; the neighboring Sail Loft houses two suites, each with cooking facilities and two small bedrooms. Grounds include a dock, ideal for launching kayaks. The

Captain's Watch B&B (207-725-0979; 916 Cundy's Harbor Rd., Harpswell) is a cupola-topped former Civil War–era hotel that now offers four spacious water-view rooms, as well as access to sailing with the innkeeper's 38-foot *Symbion II*. Other local lodging options include the Black Lantern (207-725-6165; blacklanternbandb .com; 57 Elm St.), a comfortable, moderately priced B&B on the Androscoggin River in Topsham, and Driftwood Inn and Cottages (207-833-5461; thedriftwoodinnmaine.com; 51 Washington Ave.) facing Casco Bay on Bailey Island. Open seasonally, this is a vintage-1905 compound of rustic cottages and a central lodge with a pine-walled dining room, serving breakfast and dinner. A small, saltwater

Driftwood Inn, Bailey Island   Christina Tree

swimming pool is set in the rocks. The 16 rooms vary widely in price, comfort, and view; reasonably priced house-keeping cottages are available by the week.

Local Flavors

The taste of Brunswick and the Harpswells—local restaurants, cafés, and more

Brunswick

As you might expect of Maine's premier college town, Brunswick offers widely varied and affordable dining options.

Open for Dinner Only

Clementine Restaurant (207-721-9800; clementinemaine.com; 44 Maine St.) generally gets the best high-end reviews for its sophisticated menu and white-tablecloth ambience, while Henry & Marty (207-721-9141; henry andmarty.com; 61 Maine St.) offers a welcoming atmosphere and varied menu. Back Street Bistro (backstreet bistro.net; 207-725-4060; 11 Town Place), hidden just off Maine St., is another dependable local favorite, and Bacari Bistro (207-725-2600; bacari bistro.com; 212 Maine St.) features "small plates" and is handy to the theater. Trattoria Athena (207-721-0700; trattoriaathena.wordpress.com; 25 Mill St.) serves tender goat chops, braised rabbit, and fine seafood; wild boar ragu makes a savory, brilliant sauce on zigzag-edged tender house pasta. El Camino (207-725-8228; 15 Cushing St.) is also open for dinner only but in a class of its own: funky, friendly, and widely beloved for inventive Mexican food, utilizing chemical-free seafood and meat, organic and largely local

produce. There are vegan and vegetarian options, memorable margaritas, and a wide choice of beers.

Open for Both Lunch and Dinner

The Great Impasta (207-729-5858; 42 Maine St.), just off Rt. 1, is a favorite stop for motorists as well as for local pasta lovers; plaques on booths honor regulars. Scarlet Begonias (207-721-0403) is another reasonably priced source of pastas and pizzas, also salads and overflowing sandwiches. We miss its old storefront ambience, but you are more likely to find a seat in its expanded digs at 16 Brunswick Station. For the best lunch value in town, find your way to Wild Oats Bakery and Cafe in Tontine Mall (207-725-6287), set back at 149 Maine St. With from-scratch pastries and breads, healthy build-your-own sandwiches and salads, this is the town gathering place.

A must for nostalgia buffs is the Fat Boy Drive Inn (207-729-9431; 111 Bath Rd.). This is no 1950s reconstruct but a real drive-in with carhops that's survived because it's good and reasonably priced. Spacious and informal with

Frontier Café, Brunswick   Christina Tree

Allen's Seafood, Harpswell

Christina Tree

seasonal deck dining overlooking the Androscoggin, Sea Dog Brewing (207-725-0162; seadogbrewing.com) is a good bet for families. It's housed in the vintage-1868 (former) mill, 1 Main St. in Topsham, just across the bridge, the other side of Rt. 1 from Brunswick's Maine St. Also good for families and for solo travelers in search of a comfortable place with WiFi is Frontier Café & Cinema (207-725-5222; explorefrontier.com). Housed at the back of the big brick (former) mill known as Fort Andross (14 Maine St.), it features long windows overlooking a dam and falls on the Androscoggin. The reasonably priced menu evokes different parts of the world frequented in his previous work by owner Gil Gilroy; check the website for frequent films, lectures, and events in the adjoining small theater.

The Harpswells

The Harpswells harbor numerous seasonal places to eat lobster and fresh fish by the water. The best known are Cook's Lobster House (207-833-2818) on Bailey Island and Estes Lobster House (207-833-6340), Rt. 123, South Harpswell. Both are big barns of places dating from the era of reasonably priced "shore dinners." Cook's tends to be more crowded and a shade pricier; in July and August try to get there before noon, when the Casco Bay liner arrives with its load of day-trippers from Portland. Estes is thriving under present ownership by the Morse family, who also now operate Morse's at Holbrooks (207-729-9050) in Cundy's Harbor. Allen's Seafood (207-833-2828; 119 Lookout Point Rd., Harpswell), a longtime seafood wholesaler, has added a takeout menu and picnic benches to take advantage of the glorious view. The steamed clams are locally picked and processed on the spot, served with broth and butter. The lobster couldn't be fresher. The Dolphin Chowder House (207-833-6000; dolphinmarinaandrestaurant.com; 515 Basin Point Rd.) is 2.5 miles off Rt. 123 in South Harpswell—but that doesn't seem to prevent everyone from finding it. The Saxton family's long-established restaurant, overlooking a small but busy harbor, is known for its chowders and lobster stew. The dining room fills early for both lunch and dinner; options include everything from sandwiches to sirloin, and everything comes with blueberry muffins.

Bath

Check out these great attractions, activities, and accommodations . . .

Most communities retain the best of what they build, but all the biggest and most magnificent structures built in Bath have sailed away. Over the years some 5,000 vessels were built here. Most would have towered high above the present mellow, brick downtown and striking Italianate, Greek, and Georgian Revival mansions lining Washington and High streets.

Still towering above the city, the one landmark visible from Rt. 1 is Bath Iron Works' 400-foot-high red-and-white construction crane, proclaiming the city's ongoing shipbuilding status.

American shipbuilding began downriver from Bath in 1607, with the launch of the Popham Colony's 30-ton pinnace *Virginia*. It peaked during the post–Civil War era during which 80 percent of this country's full-rigged ships were built in Maine, almost half in Bath. Obviously this is the place for a museum about ships and shipbuilding, and the Maine Maritime Museum (mainemaritimemuseum.org) fills the bill magnificently (see the sidebar). Allow an hour to entire day, especially if you take the trolley tour of the (now) General Dynamics Bath Iron Works (gdbiw.com), one of a number of tour, cruise, and paddle options offered by this lively, family-friendly museum.

From Rt. 1 the exit ramp to downtown Bath slants steeply down to the Kennebec River, just before the wide, soaring Sagadahoc Bridge. The rehabbed, brick Bath Railway Station (207-442-7291; visitbath.com) here houses a friendly information center with restrooms and useful local maps. The Maine Maritime Museum is a few minutes south along Washington St.—but be forewarned that the museum at this writing offers no place to eat. There are plenty of options in downtown Bath, where Front St. is also chockablock with antiques and clothing shops. Check out both floors of Renys (renys.com), carrying a wide selection of discounted wares, from lawn chairs to stationery, toys, and Maine specialty foods. Halcyon Yarn (halcyonyarn.com; 12 School St.) is a mecca for knitters, spinners, and rug hookers, with yarns distributed worldwide. Given its choice of dining and central location, Bath makes a good base. The Inn at Bath (207-443-4294; innatbath.com; 969 Washington St.), a restored 1830s mansion in the city's historic district, is the best place to stay. The Chocolate Church Arts Center (207-442-8455; chocolate churcharts.org; 804 Washington St.) offers frequent entertainment. The big event here is Bath Heritage Days, a multiday extravaganza surrounding the Fourth of July. Highlights: an old-time parade, guided tours, live entertainment, fun competitions, and fireworks over the Kennebec.

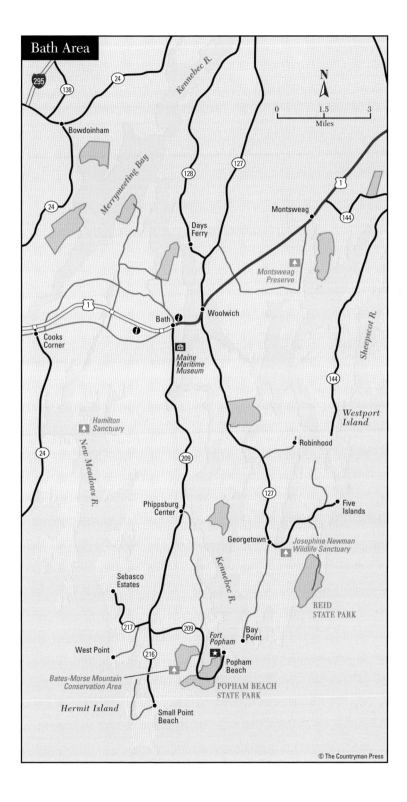

Bath Area

© The Countryman Press

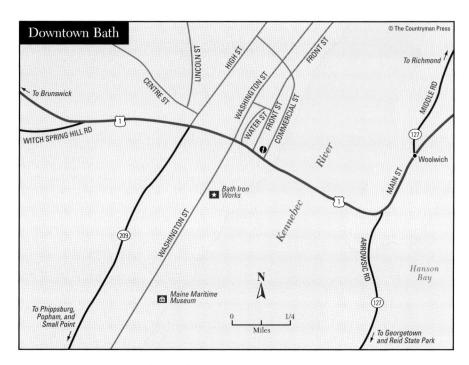

Downtown Bath

© The Countryman Press

Note: It's possible to be car-free in Bath. Arrive via the Eastern Maine Railroad and take advantage of the Bath Trolley, which circulates around town, stopping frequently at the station and the Maine Maritime Museum; $1.

Local Flavors

The taste of Bath—local restaurants, cafés, and more

The high-end dinner spot here is Solo Bistro (207-443-3373; solobistro.com; 128 Front St.). The Scandinavian decor is contemporary, and so, too, is the chef's way with locally sourced ingredients. The menu changes monthly, but there's always a wide choice, from a burger to a three-course, prix fixe menu. Beale Street Barbeque and Grill (207-442-9514; mainebbq.com; 215 Water St.), open for lunch and dinner, is known far and wide for its Tennesee-style pulled pork, ribs, and Reubens. Kennebec Tavern and Marina (207-442-9636; kennebectavern

.com; 119 Commercial St.), open for lunch and dinner, is a spacious oasis with booths and tables overlooking the Kennebec River, plus a seasonal waterside deck. The menu is large, reasonably priced, and can hit the spot after a day of driving. At Mae's Café (207-442-8577; maescafeandbakery.com; 160 Center St.) breakfast omelets are available all day and the luncheon salads and specials have a loyal following. For a quick lunch, pick up a sandwich at the Starlight Café (122 Front St.; closed weekends) and carry it down to a bench on Commercial St. overlooking the water. Café Crème (56 Front St.) offers espresso, snacks, and WiFi. The Cabin (552 Washington Ave.) is a justly popular local gathering spot for first-rate pizza in the evening; lunchtime tends to be crowded with workers from the Bath Iron Works across the road. Byrnes Irish Pub (207-443-6776; byrnesirishpub.com; 38 Centre St.) and the Admiral Steakhouse (207-443-2555; admiralsteakhouse.com; 768 Washington St.), both under the same ownership, round out dining and drinking choices.

The Maine Maritime Museum

Both the **Maine Maritime Museum** (207-443-1316; mainemaritimemuseum.org; 243 Washington St.) and **Bath Iron Works** (gdbiw.com) are sited on a 4-mile-long reach of the tidal Kennebec River, with banks sloping at precisely the right gradient for laying keels. Open 9:30–5 daily, the museum's extensive, 10-acre-plus campus includes the brick-and-glass Maritime History Building and the Percy & Small Shipyard, the country's only surviving wooden shipbuilding yard. The permanent collection of artwork, artifacts, and documents totals more than 20,000 pieces. The pride of Bath, you learn, were the Down Easters, a compromise between the clipper ship and old-style freighter that plied the globe between the 1870s and 1890s, and the mammoth multimasted schooners designed to ferry coal and local exports like ice, granite, and lime. Two sleek sculptures depict the hull and stern of the six-masted *Wyoming*, the largest wooden sailing vessel ever built. Both are built to scale and spaced as far apart as they would have been on the

Maine Maritime Museum, Bath
Courtesy, Maine Maritime Museum

actual ship, which was built on this spot. Permanent exhibits include Distant Lands of Palm and Spice, a fascinating and occasionally horrifying glimpse of where and why Maine ships sailed. Exhibits aside, the museum involves visitors in the significance of its surroundings. You can choose from a dozen cruises and other tours; reserve ahead for the popular trolley tour of the BIW shipyard in which naval vessels are currently built and repaired. There is plenty here for children, including a hands-on pilothouse and pirate-boat climbing structure. Check the website for frequent workshops and special events.

Trolley tour of Bath Iron Works
Courtesy, Maine Maritime Museum

Phippsburg Peninsula and Popham Beach

Attractions, activities, accommodations, eateries, etc.

From the Maine Maritime Museum drive south on Rt. 209, down the narrow peninsula that's the town of Phippsburg (phippsburg.com). You cross Winnegance Creek, an ancient shortcut between Casco Bay and the Kennebec River, and just beyond it, at 39 Main Rd., Up the Creek (207-442-8239; kayakingrentals.com) offers reasonably priced kayak rentals as well as access to an ideal paddling spot.

At the Phippsburg Center Store (a picnic source) be sure to turn left onto Parker Hill Rd., which puts you almost instantly in Phippsburg Center. On your left is one Maine's most oldest and most imposing mansions, while beyond lies a classic white-clapboard church shaded by a giant, ancient linden tree. The cupola-topped four-square mansion, onetime home of Maine's first U.S. congressman, is now the 1774 Inn at Phippsburg (207-389-1774; 1774inn.com), a great place to stay. Its original woodwork and airy feel have been gracefully, unstuffily restored, and the grounds slope to the river. Follow this road down the east side of the peninsula and at the junction with Rt. 209 turn left. Note the entrance to Popham Beach State Park (hotline: 207-389-9125) with 3 miles of sand. The beach width varies with the tide but there is plenty of room here to walk: 519 acres and full facilities. Rt. 209 ends shortly beyond the state park, roughly 15 miles south of Bath, at Fort Popham, a granite Civil War–era fort (with picnic benches) at the mouth of the Kennebec River. A wooded road, walking only, leads to 20th-century

1774 Inn at Phippsburg

Christina Tree

Spinney's Restaurant, Popham Beach
Christina Tree

fortifications in Fort Baldwin Memorial Park; a six-story tower offers views upriver and out to sea.

Popham Beach actually extends right to Fort Popham; access is free, but parking is limited. Much of it belongs to Spinney's Restaurant (207-389-1122), the other attraction at the end of this road, with tables (if you're lucky) on the glassed-in beachside porch. Spinney's is all about fresh fish and seafood—fried, broiled, in chowder and/or rolls. Locals avoid the crowds and duck around the corner to Percy's General Store (207-289-2010), where a back room offers water-view booths, good from breakfast on through lobster dinners.

There are two roads less taken in Phippsburg. From Rt. 209, Sebasco Rd. accesses the western side of the peninsula. Near this junction North Creek Farm (northcreekfarm.org) is an extensive nursery and perennial garden specializing in roses, also a great spot for lunch. Sebasco Harbor Resort (sebasco.com) down the road offers golf and more than 130 rooms, divided among its main lodge, annexes, and 22 cottages on scattered on 550 acres. Weddings and reunions are specialties. Facilities include tennis courts, a large swimming pool, a full children's program, adult activities, and a spa. Hidden away on a point within but beyond this resort, albeit with access to all its facilities, is Rock Gardens Inn (rockgardensinn.com), the century-old core of the entire Sebasco compound. Its 10 artfully furnished and positioned cottages and a small lodge with a dining and common space are also geared to families, but in June, July, and September many guests are here for the widely respected Sebasco Art Workshops. Still another gem hidden away down the road (turn off onto Black Landing Rd.) is Anna's Water's Edge (207-389-1803). Sited on a commercial wharf, with informal dining inside and out, this is a local favorite for steamed lobster and clams as well as a full menu (reservations accepted).

Phippsburg's other road less taken leads to Small Point, which defines the eastern rim of Casco Bay. The leg-

The dock at Rock Gardens Inn
Christina Tree

A cottage at Rock Gardens Inn, Phippsburg

Christina Tree

endary beaches here are mostly private, but unspoiled Sewall Beach is accessible by foot through the Morse Mountain Preserve (morseriver.com) from Rt. 216. Hermit Island Campground (hermitisland.com), with beach and a number of waterside tent sites, is a beloved phenomenon with a loyal following.

The Osprey Restaurant, Robinhood Marine Center

Christina Tree

Arrowsic/Georgetown

Attractions, activities, accommodations, eateries, etc.

Just east of the Sagadahoc Bridge, at the Dairy Queen that's been there forever, turn south onto Rt. 127. Cross a shorter bridge and you are on Arrowsic Island. Half a dozen miles south another short bridge puts you both in and on Georgetown, the name of the town and the island, one that's generally considered part of the larger peninsula.

The dining-out crowd turns off Rt. 127 onto Robinhood Rd., named—if

Five Islands Farm   Christina Tree

you believe it—for a local Indian chief. The area's most famous restaurant is here, the Robinhood Free Meetinghouse (207-371-2188; robinhoodmeetinghouse.com). A former 1855 chapel with 10-foot-high windows is now its main dining room; there's also a ground-floor room with a cozier feel. Prices are high but so is the quality (reservations advised). Hidden away in the Robinhood Marine Center (robinhoodmarinecenter.com), farther down the road, The Osprey Restaurant (207-371-2530) is another local dining destination with a varied menu and water views.

The big shopping destination on Rt. 127, some 9 miles south of Rt. 1, is Georgetown Pottery (georgetownpottery.com). While there are branches elsewhere, this showroom is worth a drive, with an extensive selection of practical, hand-painted pottery that's created right here.

Reid State Park, Georgetown   Christina Tree

Five Islands Dock

Christina Tree

Coveside B&B, Five Islands   Christina Tree

Rt. 127 curves east across the island and then splits. Here Seguinland Rd. leads to Reid State Park (207-371-2303), with nearly 2 miles of beach, dunes, marsh, ledges, and ocean, also a saltwater lagoon, good for small children. There's plenty of room here for everyone; parking areas and facilities are widely spaced among Half Mile, Mile, and East Beaches. Guests at local B&Bs can take advantage of free passes and their hosts' advice on where to find the least frigid water.

Fourteen miles from Rt. 1, Rt. 127 ends at a commercial lobster wharf and Five Islands Lobster and Grill (207-371-2990; fiveislandslobster.com). It's all outdoors and all about steamed lobsters and clams with corn and potatoes, lobster rolls, and fried seafood (BYOB). Just up the road look for Five Islands Farm (fiveislandsfarm.com), a small shingled emporium selling wines, local produce, and one of the region's largest selections of Maine artisinal cheeses. The gold at the end of this rainbow is, however, Coveside Bed and Breakfast (207-371-2807; covesidebandb.com). Tucked into a corner of quiet Gotts Cove, this is an exceptional hideaway with seven bright, comfortable rooms with water views. Sumptuous breakfasts are served, weather permitting, on a flower-filled patio above a lawn that slopes invitingly to shaded Adirondack chairs on the shore. You won't want to leave.

4

Damariscotta Region

INCLUDING WISCASSET AND PEMAQUID

The 7 miles of Rt. 1 between Wiscasset and Damariscotta access some of the most varied and rewarding stretches of shoreline along the entire coast. In summer months, to the annoyance of motorists bent on making time, the stretch is also a major speed bump. Wiscasset is the first coastal town (heading northeast) that Rt. 1 runs right through. It looks like a great place to stop, and many do. That turns them into pedestrians, who cross back and forth among the village's antiques shops and restaurants, which in turn annoys other motorists. Traffic can back up in both directions, for miles.

Once across the Sheepscot River on Wiscasset's wide new bridge—which was supposed to have solved the traffic snarl—many cars turn down Rt. 27, following it 10 miles south, down the spine of a peninsula to Boothbay Harbor. This is the area's liveliest resort, with the lion's share of lodging options. Often, however, these can be booked more solidly in August than nearby, less-touristed communities.

Rt. 1 bypasses downtown Damariscotta, but nobody should. The brick main street is a gem with great shopping and dining. It's the gateway to a small region with a large, quiet lake and long tidal rivers. Stretching south from Damariscotta, the Pemaquid Peninsula is known for its famous lighthouse. There's much more there, however: busy working lobstering harbors at Round Pond and New Harbor, boatbuilding in Bristol, and yachting at Christmas Cove.

This historic, visitor-friendly village is an obvious way stop. The places to eat are varied and good, antiques stores abound, and the historic buildings are beautiful. We usually avoid the worst of the seasonal traffic by ducking off Rt. 1 before it becomes Main St. Turn down Lee St. and follow it down to Fore St. and Water St. Here Waterfront Park offers parking and restrooms.

Wiscasset

Attractions, activities, accommodations, eateries, etc.

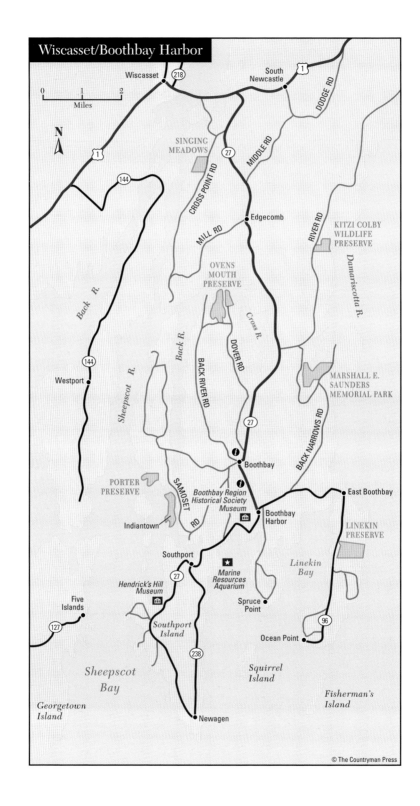

Red's Eats, Wiscasset   Christina Tree

Since food is usually the first point of interest here, let's begin with the obvious: Red's Eats. The lineup at this legendary food stand (just before the bridge) is frequently long, and the seating at its picnic tables is limited, but Red's lobster rolls pack an entire lobster and consistently get raves, as do the fried clams and hot dogs. Theres no legend and usually no line at Sprague's Lobster (207-882-7814) across the road. Never mind that its deck is right on the river and the lobster rolls are generous and fresh; there are also crab rolls and really good clam fritters. The weatherproof, year-round place to eat here is Sarah's (207-822-7504; sarahscafe.com), corner of Main and Water, with seasonal outdoor seating. The menu is extensive, featuring pizza, chowders, salads, and lobster more than 15 different ways. Down Water St., Le Garage (207-882-5409; legarage.com) is frequently less crowded at lunch (try a seafood crêpe) than restaurants on the main drag, and it's the preferred choice for dinner. Specialties include traditional creamed finnan haddie, charbroiled native lamb, and chicken pie. Reserve a table on the porch. South of town on Rt. 1 The Sea Basket (207-882-6581) is also a dependable stop, known for its lobster stew. If you just want to pick up a picnic and push on, then Treats (207-882-9192; 80 Main St.) fills your bill with terrific sandwiches you can take along to the Sherman Lake Rest Area, 4 miles up Rt. 1. There picnic tables overlook a tidal river (it was a lake until the dam broke), and there are spiffy new restrooms. But we suggest you linger longer in Wiscasset.

Still the shire town of Lincoln County, Wiscasset is only half as populous as it was in its shipping heyday—which, judging from the town's clapboard mansions, began after the Revolution and ended around the time of the Civil War. Lincoln County Courthouse, built in 1824 on the town common, is the oldest functioning courthouse in New England. At one point, it's claimed, Wiscasset was the busiest international port north of Boston.

The town's early-19th-century mansions certainly reflect great wealth. Two of these, Castle Tucker at Lee and High streets and the Nickels-Sortwell House, 122 Main St., are both open for tours seasonally on weekends (historicnewengland .org). The 32-room Musical Wonder House (207-882-7163; musicalwonderhouse .com; 18 High St.) houses some 5,000 music boxes as well as a collection of player grand pianos and organs, spring-wound phonographs, music birds, and much more. By contrast the town's other attraction, the Old Lincoln Country Jail and Museum (207-882-6317; 133 Federal St., Rt. 218), is a chilling vintage-1813 model, in use until 1930.

From Wiscasset, Rt. 27 runs northwest to Dresden Mills. From there it's just a few miles to the haunting Pownalborough Court House (207-882-6817), a three-story throwback to 1761. Rt. 218 veers northeast, paralleling the Sheepscot River through backcountry to Head Tide Village and Alna, home of the Wiscasset, Waterville & Farmington Railway (207-882-4193; wwfry.org) with its narrow-gauge excursion train.

West of Wiscasset Rt. 144 heads winds down quiet Westport Island. It's 8 miles to the Squire Tarbox Inn (207-882-7693; squiretarboxinn.com; 1181 Main Rd., Westport), a Federal-era farmhouse offering both destination dining and lodging. "A good country inn should be tasted," maintains Swiss innkeeper-chef Mario De Pietro. Dining is in a former summer kitchen with a large colonial fireplace and ceiling timbers that were once part of ship; in summer there's also a screened deck. The menu is classic Continental but with signature Swiss specialties and, always, delicious roesti potatoes. Ingredients are local, with strawberries, greens, and many vegetables from the inn's own organic farm. The parlor and four largest guest rooms in the "new" (1825) part of the house all have working fireplaces; seven more rustic rooms are in a converted 1820s carriage

Wiscasset, Waterville & Farmington Railway
Christina Tree

Squire Tarbox Inn, Westport

barn. The extensive grounds include a walking path and farm (with goats and chickens); amenities include mountain bikes and a rowboat.

The place to stay in middle of the village of Wiscasset itself **Marston House** (207-882-6010; marstonhouse.com) at the corner of Main and Middle streets Its two guest rooms, each with private entrance and working fireplace, are in the carriage barn, back behind an antiques shop specializing in early American textiles and furnishings. **Snow Squall Inn** (207-882-6892; snowsquallinn.com; 5 Bradford Rd.) is south of town, set back from Rt. 1. It's a comfortably elegant 1850s house named for a clipper ship. There's an unusual amount of common space as well as four air-conditioned guest rooms in the main house, and three 2-room suites in the Carriage House. **Highnote** (207-882-9628; wiscasset.net/highnote; 26 Lee St.) is a high-Victorian mansion with a shared bath, reasonable rates, and European-style breakfasts.

The Boothbays

Check out these great attractions and activities . . .

In the village of Boothbay Harbor water is more than a view. You cross it—via a footbridge—to get from one side of town to the other, and you can explore it on a wide choice of excursion boats and in sea kayaks. It is obvious from the very lay of this old fishing village that its people have always gotten around on foot or in boats. Though parking has increased in recent years, it's still a challenge. Cars feel like an intrusion.

Boats are what all three of the Boothbays have traditionally been about. Boats are built, repaired, and sold in East Boothbay and Southport. Boat excursions range from an hour-long sail around the outer harbor to a 90-minute crossing (each way) to Monhegan Island. Fishermen can pursue giant tuna, stripers, and blues, and nature lovers can cruise out to see seals, whales, and puffins.

In the middle of summer Boothbay Harbor itself is chockablock full of tourists licking ice cream cones, chewing freshly made taffy and fudge, browsing in shops, looking into art galleries, listening to band concerts on the library lawn, and, of course, eating lobster. You get the feeling it's been like this every summer since the 1870s.

On your way into town stop by the Boothbay Harbor Chamber of Commerce (207-633-2353; boothbayharbor.com) information center just before the lights at the junction of Rt. 27 with Rt. 96. Pick up a map locating parking lots; you can also get printed directions to key attractions. East Boothbay is a left onto Rt. 96 at the lights and the harbor is straight ahead, but Boothbay Harbor is complicated.

Shopping on the library lawn   Christina Tree

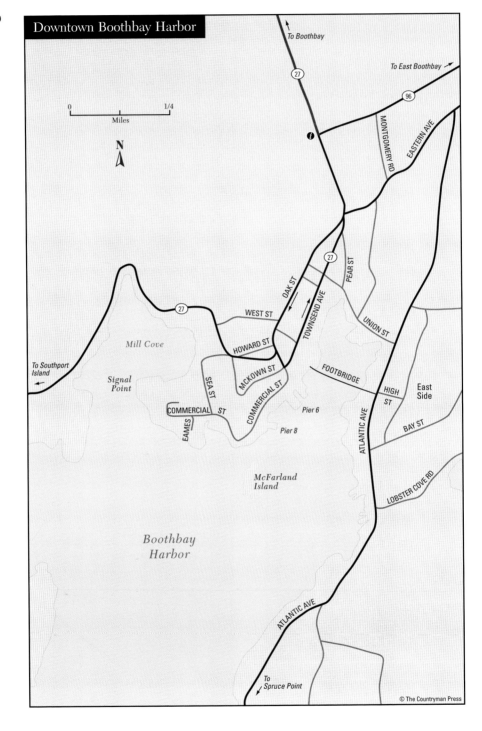

Downtown Boothbay Harbor

To Boothbay

27

To East Boothbay

96

MONTGOMERY RD

EASTERN AVE

0   1/4
Miles

N

PEAR ST

OAK ST

TOWNSEND AVE

UNION ST

WEST ST

HOWARD ST

Mill Cove

FOOTBRIDGE

To Southport
Island

Signal
Point

SEA ST

MCKOWN ST

COMMERCIAL ST

HIGH
ST

East
Side

COMMERCIAL   ST

EAMES

Pier 6

ATLANTIC AVE

BAY ST

Pier 8

McFarland
Island

LOBSTER COVE RD

Boothbay
Harbor

ATLANTIC AVE

To
Spruce Point

© The Countryman Press

Many lodging places and restaurants are on Atlantic Ave. on the east side of the harbor; from there quiet roads run out to Spruce Point and around Linekin Bay. Rt. 27 continues out the other end of the village toward Southport Island.

Thanks to the fervor of developers from the 1870s on, the Boothbay coastline is distinguished by the quantity of its summer cottages, many of which can be rented by the week, even in old summer compounds like Capitol and Squirrel Islands. Many of these classic "Maine rustic cottages," some quite large, line Shore Dr. along Ocean Point at the end of Rt. 96. With so many families on board in summer you'll find a wide choice of drop-in activities for kids. The obvious family attractions are Boothbay Railway Village (207-633-4727; railwayvillage.com) on Rt. 27, 3 miles north of the harbor; the Kenneth Stoddard Shell Museum (207-6333-4828; Hardwick Rd.), exhibiting one of the world's largest private collections of seashells; and the Maine State Aquarium (207-633-9559; maine.gov/dmr/rm/aquarium), at the end of McKown Point Rd., where tanks are filled with sea creatures from Maine waters, from alewives to a 17-pound lobster.

The area's single biggest attraction these days is the Coastal Maine Botanical Gardens (207-633-4333; mainegardens.org), back up Rt. 27 to the common in Boothbay, then out Barter's Island Rd. This 250-acre spread includes a visitors center with a gift shop and café, surrounded by a kitchen garden, a children's garden inspired by children's books, a rose garden, and the Garden of the Five Senses. Native species, more than 350, represent the majority of plantings. Wooded paths lead down through a series of gardens to a the Shoreline Trail. It's not difficult to spend the better part of a day here.

Thanks to the Boothbay Region Land Trust (207-63-4818; bbrlt.org; 137 Townsend Ave.), there are now also easily accessible waterside preserves with many miles of trails meandering through hundreds of acres of spruce and pine, down to smooth rocks and tidal pools. Pick up a brochure and map (showing 30 miles of trails) to the easily accessible properties. The 1,700 acres of land under the trust's protection include Porter Preserve, with 23 wooded acres, including a beach, on Barters Island not far beyond the botanical gardens.

Sooner rather than later we suggest that you get out on the water. Check out the lineup of boat excursion companies along the piers in Boothbay Harbor and reserve seats on those that appeal to you. At least visit the Burnt Island Light Station; in July and August guides portray the family who lived there in the 1950s. It's a 15-minute boat ride from Pier 8. Balmy Days Cruises (207-633-2284; balmyday cruises.com/lighthouse) also offers harbor and coastal tours, mackerel fishing, day sails, and—the biggie—a day trip to Monhegan Island. At Pier 1 Cap'n Fish Boat Cruises (207-633-3244; mainewhales.com) specializes in

Boothbay Harbor offers plenty of ways to get out on the water. *Christina Tree*

whale-watching trips, but they also offer a wide variety of cruises including a puffin-watching cruise around Egg Rock off Pemaquid and trap-pulling from a lobster boat. Schooner *Lazy Jack* (207-633-3444; sailsschoonerlazy jack.com) also offers two-hour sails, departing Pier 1. If you'd rather paddle your way along the shoreline, sign on for a tour with Tidal Transit Company (207-633-7140; kayakboothbay .com; 18 Granary Way). A number of deep-sea charters are also based here.

Boothbay Harbor is a good shopping town.
Christina Tree

Boothbay Harbor offers its share of quality shops. Long-standing landmarks include House of Logan (207-633-2293; 20 Townsend Ave.), with traditional men's and women's clothing, and its companion store, The Village Store and Children's Shop, selling gifts and furnishings at 34 Townsend Ave. Sherman's Book & Stationery Store (800-371-8128; shermans.com; 5 Commercial St) is a two-story emporium filled with souvenirs, kitchenware, games, and art supplies as well as books, specializing in nautical titles. Don't miss The Palabra Shop

The Shore Path at Ocean Point is a great place to picnic.
Christina Tree

(207-633-4225; palabrashop.com; 53 Commercial St.), a warren of 10 rooms offering everything from kitschy souvenirs to handcrafts and jewelry to a few antiques. Upstairs (open by appointment) is a Poland Spring Museum. The peninsula's most famous shop is back up on Rt. 27: Edgecomb Potters (207-882-9493; edgecombpotters.com; 727 Boothbay Rd.) is a two-tiered gallery filled with deeply colored pots, vases, lamps, bowls, cookware, and jewelry. There's also a small seconds corner and a sculpture garden.

The harbor is home to upward of a dozen art galleries, including Gold/Smith Gallery (207-633-6252; 41 Commercial St.), Gleason Fine Art (207-633-6849; gleasonfineart.com; 31 Townsend Ave.), and allen david Gallery (207-633-0003; allendavidgallery.com; 15 Townsend Ave.). Another dozen-plus are scattered along the shore from Ocean Point to Southport Island, all holding open studio on first Fridays, June–Oct.

Whether they're looking for art shops, galleries, beaches, or shore paths, visitors sooner or later find their way out Rt. 96 to East Boothbay, a small village that's home to a big boatyard. The East Boothbay General Store (207-633-7800) is a great source of morning doughnuts, unusual pizzas, and sandwiches to take on down to Ocean Point for a picnic on the beach or shore path. It's also a must to cross the Townsend Gut swing bridge to Southport Island. Head down Beach Rd. to the beach or all the way down Rt. 27 to Newagen with its smooth rocks overlooking the entrance to Sheepscot Bay. It was this landscape that inspired Rachel Carson, who first summered on the peninsula in 1946, to write much of *The Edge of the Sea* (1955) and then *Silent Spring* (1962), the book that changed global thinking about human beings' relation to basic laws of nature.

When the sun sets, everyone from every corner of this region seems to converge on Boothbay Harbor's boardwalk and the many restaurants that are never enough in high season. Don't miss out on the Down East Ice Cream Factory (207-633-3016), with great flavors like Perry's Nut House. It's around the corner from the log-sided, vintage-1929 Romar Bowling Lanes (207-633-5721) and the Daffy, Taffy and Fudge Factory. Nearby entertainment options include dinner and musical reviews at the Carousel Music Theater (207-633-5297), as well as live performances at the Opera House (207-633-5159; operahouse.com) and Boothbay Playhouse (207-633-3379; boothbayplayhouse.com).

Topside Inn, Boothbay Harbor   Nancy English

Checking In

Best places to stay in the Boothbays

For anyone who wants to stay within walking distance of the Boothbay Harbor village action, Topside Inn (207-633-5404; topsideinn.com; 60

McKown St.) is the pick. It's sited atop McKown Hill, a quiet island above the hubbub, with views west to the sunset over the water and islands. Rooms are divided between the handsome 1876 mansion with its common space and breakfast room, and a pair of two-story motel-style annexes with back balconies facing the water. Another great location is the Five Gables Inn (207-633-4551; fivegablesinn.com; 107 Murray Hill Rd.) in East Boothbay. Sited across from a quiet waterside byway, it's not far from Ocean Point on one hand and the harbor on the other. Its 16 rooms (15 with a bay view) are imaginatively, comfortably furnished; 5 have a working fireplace (the smaller third-floor gable rooms offer some of the best views of the water). Guests meet and mingle in the spacious, cheerful common room with its large hearth, and along the veranda. Many are repeats, familiar with longtime

On the veranda at Five Gables, East Boothbay
Christina Tree

hosts De and Mike Kennedy; a Culinary Institute of America graduate, Mike prides himself on the extensive

Swim or sail at Linekin Bay.

Christina Tree

breakfast buffet. Hodgdon Island Inn (207-633-7474; hodgdonislandinn.com; 374 Barter's Island Rd., Boothbay)—one of the few places here open year-round—is also in a seemingly out-of-the-way spot but not really. It's a mile beyond the botanical gardens, overlooking a quiet cove and hand-cranked drawbridge, and handy to the preserves on Barter's Island. The nine air-conditioned rooms have water views, and a heated swimming pool is set in the landscaped garden.

The Boothbays are also home to several seasonal, full-service, long-established resorts. The largest and toniest is Spruce Point Inn Resort & Spa (207-633-4152; sprucepointinn .com; 88 Grandview Ave.), set in 57 landscaped acres on a peninsula jutting into Boothbay Harbor. Rooms are divided among the 1890s Main Inn with splendid views, contemporary lodges, Woodland Condominiums, and vintage cottages. Facilities abound and include a full-service spa (weddings are a specialty) and a children's program in July and August. At the tip of South-port Island, Newagen Seaside Inn (207-633-5242; newagenseasideinn .com) has a more traditional and remote feel, and a loyal following. The original inn, which reminds us of a Connecticut mansion in a 1940s Kate Hepburn movie, houses traditional guest rooms and suites as well as com-mon space; there are also junior suites with cooking facilities and the Little Inn, plus a scattering of classic cot-tages. Facilities include a heated fresh-water pool and tennis courts. Best of all is the shore path along the rocks, beneath the pines. Ocean Point Inn 207-633-4200 or 800-552-5554; ocean pointinn.com; 191 Shore Rd., East Boothbay) is an informal, moderately priced complex of 61 rooms, suites, cottages, and apartments with a heated

pool and Adirondack chairs overlooking the ocean. Ocean Point's shore path and beach are close by. Last but not least is Linekin Bay Resort (207-633-2494; linekinbayresort.com; 92 Wall Point Rd.), a century-old, family-geared compound tucked into a quiet cove, with a focus on sailing. The five "lodges" and 35 rustic cabins are set along the shore, backed by pines on 20 shoreline acres. Rates include three meals in high season as well as use of the Rhodes 19 sailboats (lessons are available), kayaks, tennis, and more. June and September B&B rates are surprisingly reasonable.

Boothbay Harbor has more than its share of large waterside motor inns, but for these we defer to the AAA and Mobile guides. In the harbor we do recommend the Flagship Inn (207-633-5094; boothbaylodging.com; 200 Townsend Ave.). It's open year-round and affordable, with air-conditioning and a swimming pool. On Rt. 238, Southport Island, the rates at the sea-sonal Ship Ahoy Motel (207-633-5222; shipahoymotel.com) are unbeatable. This is a family-owned motel with 54 tidy units, all with TV and air-conditioning, 30 with a private balcony right on the water, others tucked into the granite ledges and pines. Facilities include an unheated pool, coffee shop, and dock. Check with the chamber of commerce for several prime local sources for vacation rentals.

Local Flavors

The taste of the Boothbays—local restaurants, cafés, and more

Ports of Italy (207-633-1011; portsof italy.com; 47 Commercial St.) is the high-end preferred dining spot on the harbor. The pasta is homemade, the Italian flavors are genuine, and the upstairs dining room is bright, with a lovely outside area, weather permitting. The risotto is studded with seafood and the zabaglione, with strawberries or blueberries. At The Boat House Bistro (207-633-0400; theboathousebistro .com; 12 The By-Way) it's the same extensive, largely tapas-style menu both for lunch and dinner, served in any of the dining rooms on three floors; the open rooftop deck offers the best water views. Lunch on wild mushroom ragu simmered in cognac cream, served with crispy polenta and Gruyère cheese and dine on a choice of seafood paellas. The Rocktide Inn (207-633-4455; rocktideinn.com; 35 Atlantic Ave.) is worth a visit, if just to see its ships models and have a drink in the tiki-style, waterside On-the-Rocks lounge; the main dining room decor and menu are traditional. The area's resort inn dining rooms—Bogie's Hideaway at Spruce Point Inn, the Cape Harbor Grill at Newagen Seaside Inn, and the dining room at Linekin Bay Resort—are all known for dependably fine dining.

The fact is that it's lobster most folks are here to eat, and the simpler, the better. The Lobster Dock (207-633-7120; thelobsterdock.com; 49 Atlantic Ave.) at the east end of the footbridge gets top rating for lobster rolls, either hot with drawn butter or cold with a dab of mayo, as well as lobster and shore dinners or prime rib. Crabcakes are a specialty. Robinson's Wharf (207-633-3830; robinsons wharf.net) on Southport Island, just across Townsend Gut from Boothbay Harbor, is the other sure winner. On a sunny day sit on the dock at one of the picnic tables and watch the boats unload their catch. Choices include lobsters and lobster rolls, fried shrimp, clams, scallops, fish chowder,

lobster stew, sandwiches, and homemade desserts. There is also the Clambake at Cabbage Island (207-633-7200; cabbageislandclambakes .com), a long-standing tradition. The clambake includes lobsters, clams, corn, and potatoes steamed in seaweed then served on picnic tables. In bad weather a circa-1900 lodge seats up to 100 people by a huge fireplace. The charge includes the boat ride to the harbor island from Fisherman's Wharf.

Boothbay Harbor offers a number of places for a satisfying lunch or reasonably priced dinner. Our favorite lunch spot is Ebb Tide (207-633-5692) on Commercial St., open all day, year-round. Nothing fancy but airconditioning, knotty-pine booths, and breakfast all day, plus lobster rolls, club sandwiches, fisherman's platters, reasonably priced specials, and homemade desserts like peach shortcake. Blue Moon Café (207-633-2220; blue moonboothbayharbor.com; 54 Commercial St.) is a little café with a seaside deck, good for crabcakes and fresh greens. Chowder House (207-633-5761; chowderhouseinc.com; Granary Way beside the footbridge) has a waterfront deck and a menu that includes chowders, crab rolls, grilled ribs, and a full bar. 89 Baker's Way (207-633-1119; 89 Townsend Ave.) is just the place for fried apple dumpling, you think, and then you smell lemongrass cooking and wonder where you are. There are two worlds here: a full bakery, and a restaurant that serves traditional, reasonably priced Vietnamese foods. McSeagulls (207-633-5900; mcseagullsonline.com; 14 Wharf St.) offers wharfside dining and can get crazy packed in high season. It's a local gathering place offseason because it's good. Try the lobster with northern white beans.

Get a table on the deck at Lobsterman's Wharf, East Boothbay.

Christina Tree

In East Boothbay, Lobsterman's Wharf (207-633-3443; lobstermans wharf.com; 224 Ocean Point Rd.) offers plenty of inside seating, but the prime spots are on the deck with a view of yachts and tugboats at the neighboring boatyard. Get there early.

Damariscotta/ Pemaquid Peninsula

Check out these great attractions and activities . . .

Damariscotta's musical name means "meeting place of the alewives," and in spring spawning alewives can indeed be seen climbing more than 40 feet up a fish ladder from Great Salt Bay to the fresh water in Damariscotta Lake.

The area's first residents also found an abundance of oysters here, judging from the shells they heaped over the course of 2,400 years on opposite banks of the river just below Salt Bay. Native Americans also had a name for the peninsula jutting 10 miles seaward from this spot: *Pemaquid* means "long finger." At one tip of this finger stands Pemaquid Light (lighthousefoundation.org), pictured on Maine's quarter as well as on countless calendars because it looks just like a lighthouse should look. It stands atop dramatic but clamber-friendly rocks. These are composed of varied seams of granite schist and softer volcanic rock, ridged in ways that invite climbing, and pocked with tidal pools that demand stopping. The former keeper's house is now The Fisherman's Museum (207-677-2492); visitors

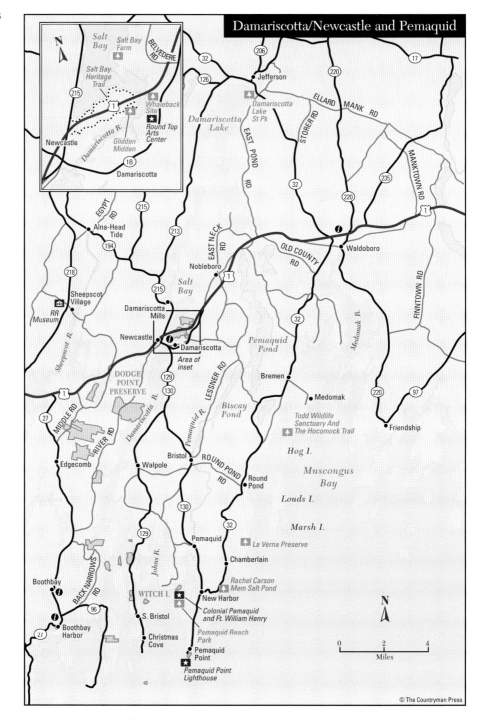

Damariscotta/Newcastle and Pemaquid

© The Countryman Press

Pemaquid Light stands atop rocks, great for clambering. Christina Tree

are welcome to climb the 39 steps inside the light itself. There are also picnic tables here above the rocks, under the pines.

Pemaquid Light has never been more famous, but the surrounding area is a shadow of the busy resort it was around the turn of the last century, when nearby New Harbor was a busy steamboat stop. Pemaquid Beach (207-677-2754), a lovely, town-owned facility, is seldom crowded. Up the road Fort William Henry, a crenellated, 1908 stone re-creation of a 17th-century tower built by the English to ward off the French, draws relatively few visitors; fewer still notice the "Rock of Pemaquid" enshrined within this tower. A century ago, however, this was a hugely popular tourist attraction, billed as the rock settlers alighted on, years before any got to Plymouth. The fort is now part of the Colonial Pemaquid Historic Site (207-677-2423; friendsofcolonialpemaquid.org) and includes a visitors center and museum depicting the layerings of history here. More than 100,000 artifacts unearthed in excavations from the neighboring field document this as a seasonal fishing station, established circa 1610 and evolving into a trading outpost circa 1630–50. Never a fully fledged settlement, the site was forgotten until 19th-century farmers began unearthing its cellar holes and, with the arrival of steamboats, created a tourist attraction. Then the steamboats stopped, numerous big wooden summer hotels closed, and "Maine's Lost City" was forgotten again, until fairly recently.

New Harbor, also right up the road from the lighthouse, is one of the coast's more historic and picturesque harbors. It's filled with lobster boats and serves as the departure point for Hardy Boat Cruises (207-677-2026; hardyboat.com) to Monhegan Island and to Eastern Rock, one of the few Maine islands on which puffins breed. Take off from Shaw's Wharf (207-677-2200), a classic lobster pound in which you select your lobster from the pool below and feed on it upstairs at picnic tables, either inside or out.

The shortest route from Damariscotta to Pemaquid Point is Rt. 130, but if time permits, find your way to Rt. 129 as it winds down the second point on the peninsula. This takes you across the drawbridge at a busy channel in South Bristol known as "the Gut," and on down to Christmas Cove with its inviting

Coveside Restaurant and Marina (207-644-8282; covesiderestaurant.com).

At the very least drive one way to or from Pemaquid Point on Rt. 32, along the eastern shore of the peninsula, with a stop at Round Pond. There on the public dock Muscongus Bay Lobster (207-529-5528) and Round Pond Lobster (207-529-5725) compete for your business. The weatherproof, famously fine place to eat here is the Anchor Inn (207-529-5584; anchorinnrestaurant.com), open daily in-season for lunch and dinner with a tiered dining room overlooking the harbor. Before leaving Round Pond, stop by the Granite Hall Store, built as a dance hall in the 1880s when this was a busy spot, now a trove of good things from penny candy to Scottish scarves and Maine-made woolens.

Granite Hall Store, Round Harbor

Christina Tree

Damariscotta is the commercial and cultural heart of this region, its solid Main St. flanked by fine brick buildings constructed after the fire of 1845, studded with shops and restaurants. This is home base for family-owned Renys (207-563-3177; renys.com) with 14 stores scattered around Maine. The original store here sells quality clothing while Renys Underground, across the street, offers everything from tea to TVs, bedding, china, toys, a wide assortment of specialty food, boots, and all manner of staples you didn't realize you needed. The antithesis of Walmart, Renys has been the subject of two Maine musicals. Across the way is the vintage Lincoln Theater (207-563-3424; lcct.org) with a renovated, elevator-accessed second floor, a venue for both films and live presentations. At street level the theater is also home to Maine Coast Bookshop & Café (207-563-3207; mainecoastbookshop.com), one of the state's outstanding independent bookstores. Parking in Damariscotta, incidentally, is far easier than it initially looks; there are ample lots behind the buildings on both sides of Main St.

For a sense of beauty of this immediate area, find your way to the

Damariscotta Main St. shops

Christina Tree

Damariscotta River Association (207-563-1393; damariscottariver.org; 110 Belvedere Rd.) headquarters at 115-acre Salt Pond Farm, 0.25 mile north of the blinking light on Rt. 1. Its hay fields and salt- and freshwater marshes are laced with walking paths. This is also the site of seasonal Friday farmer's markets; pick up a map to DRA preserves throughout the area. Families intent on warm-water swimming should follow Rt. 32 north to Damariscotta Lake State Park (207-549-7600).

Lincoln Theater, Damariscotta   Christina Tree

Checking In

Best places to stay in Damariscotta and on the Pemaquid Peninsula

The obvious places to stay in Damariscotta are actually just across the bridge in Newcastle. The Newcastle Inn (207-563-5685; newcastleinn.com; 60 River Rd.) offers 14 tasteful and comfortable rooms, some with water view, 9 with gas fireplace; grounds slope to the river overlooking the village of Damariscotta. The nearby Harborview at Newcastle (207-563-2900; theharborview.com; 34 Main St.), with just three spacious guest rooms, features a many-windowed living room and deck overlooking the harbor. Just up Rt. 215 in Damariscotta Mills the Mill Pond Inn (207-563-8014; mill pondinn.com) is a welcoming vintage-1780 house beside a millpond, an extension of Lake Damariscotta that's great for swimming. The six rooms, including a two-room suite, are so different from one another that you might want to ask for descriptions, but all are the same reasonable price. Innkeeper Bobby Weare can be persuaded to take guests down the big lake in his 16-foot restored motorboat, and to arrange fishing trips.

Down on the Pemaquid Peninsula the Inn at Round Pond (207-529-2004; theinnatroundpond.com; 1442 Rt. 32) is a delightful B&B with rooms in tasteful colors, furnished with antiques and hung with original art. A third floor and mansard roof were added to this 1830s Colonial around

Ye Olde Forte Cabins, Pemaquid Beach
Christina Tree

Mill Pond Inn

Christina Tree

the turn of the last century, when it became the Harbor View Hotel. In New Harbor the family-owned Gosnold Arms (207-677-3727; gosnold .com; 16 Rt. 32) offers 10 simple but comfortable guest rooms and 20 cottage units, 6 of them with decks, smack dab on the entrance to the harbor. The inn is steps from Shaw's Wharf, which means you can walk not just to dinner but also onto an excursion boat for a cruise to Egg Rock or Monhegan; the alternative is parking a ways up the road. The turn-of-the-last-century Bradley Inn (207-677-2105; bradley inn.com; 3063 Pemaquid Point) offers 14 rooms divided between the main house and annexes. It's the only local inn to still offer dinner as well as breakfast; amenities include a spa and clunker bicycles to take you the mile to the lighthouse. Weekly cottage rentals include the Thompson House and

Cottages (207-677-2317; thompson cottages.net) with 21 cottages sleeping up to five people, many facing New Harbor or Back Cove, all with fireplace (wood supplied). In Pemaquid Beach you'll find Ye Olde Forte Cabins (207-677-2661; yeoldefortecabins.com; 28 Old Fort Rd.), a double row of classic 1920s cabins sloping to the shore.

Local Flavors

The taste of Damariscotta—
local restaurants, cafés, and more

Damariscotta is the best place in the Northeast to eat oysters. For 2,000 years, judging from the famous shell heaps at Glidden Point and along the river, the locals have been eating oysters here. By the 1970s native oyster beds had all but disappeared due to overharvesting but, thanks to the University of Maine's Darling Marine Center on the Damariscotta River, seedlings were reintroduced. The resulting firm, distinctively sweet and salty oysters are served in the world's best restaurants. You can buy them at Glidden Point Sea Farm (207-633-3599; oysterfarm.com; 707 River Rd.) in Edgecomb or sample them at local restaurants. At the Damariscotta River Grill (207-563-2992; damariscottariver grill.com; 155 Main St.), reserve a table upstairs by the window or sit up at the copper bar. Seasonal Schooner Landing (207-563-7447; Schooner Wharf), also on Main St., features an oyster bar. At King Eider's Pub (207-563-6008; kingeiderspub.com; 2 Elm St.) you can make a meal of oysters and the other house specialty, crabcakes, washed down by a wide choice of brews.

The Salt Bay Café (207-563-3302; salt-baycafe.com; 88 Main St.) is a dependably good place with a big menu, including the widest variety of vegetarian dishes around. Newcastle Publick House (207-563-7447; 52 Main St.) across the bridge in Newcastle is an invitingly informal family-friendly pub, also a place to feast on shepherd's pie, wild mushroom fettuccine— or oysters.

5

Western Penobscot Bay

FROM WALDOBORO TO BUCKSPORT

The span of the Maine coast from the southern point of Monhegan Island, 12 miles out to sea from Port Clyde, to the town of Bucksport, just across the sweeping new Penobscot Narrows Bridge and across Verona Island, lies in a northeasterly direction. Both at its southern end and midpoints, Western Penobscot Bay holds several ferry terminals, often under siege in summer by travelers heading to the islands of Vinalhaven, North Haven, and Islesboro; the ferries operate less frequently through winter to serve the islands' year-round residents. Up the hills around Camden and down the long straightaways by Thomaston, Rt. 1 moves thousands of visitors back and forth, while the water is a highway for birds, fish, and eels.

People have always flocked to this part of the coast, no matter what kind of obstacles they encountered, from traffic jams in Wiscasset to the daily summer slowdown in Camden's stretch of Rt. 1. A fleet of Windjammers in Rockport and Camden is one enduring attraction. The sailing ships are ready to carry you to sea for a day or longer, bringing their own sense of history into the present moment as you encounter the coast from a ship's deck much like the first European settlers and traders. The Penobscot Marine Museum in Searsport shows off artifacts from that past in a historic setting and should not be missed. All the towns you pass on Rt. 1 flaunt fine 19th-century buildings, many constructed with money earned in the shipping trade by ships' captains. Some are now good bed & breakfasts, offering today's visitors historic hospitality.

Rockland is the southern center of this thriving area, its Main St. packed with good restaurants, fine shops, terrific bookshops, a renovated theater, and the flourishing Farnsworth Art Museum (207-596-6457; farnsworthmuseum.org; 16 Museum St., Rockland). The area's prime draw, the museum is open year-round: May 15–Oct. 31, Tue.–Sun. 10–5;

Waldoboro to Lincolnville Beach

Check out these great attractions and activities . . .

Sunset from the Monhegan ferry dock

Nancy English

Wed. 10–8 (free 5–8). The exhibitions—rug hooking was the one recent subject—events, and permanent collection make this museum an essential stop for art lovers.

Rockland made its money with sardine packing and fish processing, and while those businesses were vanishing, life was tough for the locals. Today, with a granite breakwater around the harbor, the packing plants vanished, the views and the air are magnificent. Visitors' dollars have gone a long way toward making up for missing industries.

Farnsworth Homestead (207-596-6457; 21 Elm St., Rockland) will tell you some of the story of the change. This home, kept precisely as it was in 1935, when its owner Lucy Farnsworth died, honors the memory of her father, who made a fortune in the local lime industry—a lime kiln can be explored at Rockport's park—and shipping. His fortune, cared for during his daughter's lifetime with some skill, was left by Lucy's will to care for her home, and to found the Farnsworth Art Museum.

The Wyeth Center in its own white, former church holds paintings and other work by three generations of the Wyeth family: N. C. Wyeth, Andrew Wyeth, and Jamie Wyeth (across the street is a Wyeth research center). The main galleries present artworks focused on the Maine landscape, from early Hudson River School painters to modern counterparts like Alex Katz. Robert Indiana's beloved *EAT* sign on the outside corner of the building has turned the whole street into a gallery.

Fort Knox and the Penobscot Observatory

Whoosh and the elevator sets you 43 stories above the Penobscot River, atop one of the two obelisk-like pylons anchoring the Waldo–Hancock bridge. This is the **Penobscot Narrows Observatory** (207-469-6553; maine.gov/observatory; open daily May–Oct. 9–5, until 6 in July, Aug.). Far below, Bucksport is a toy town, and from another window Penobscot Bay sweeps away to the horizon. This is the only bridge with an observatory in the country.

Penobscot Narrows Bridge
Nancy English

West of the bridge a traffic light on Rt. 1 eases access to the Fort Knox grounds, site of the elevator up to the observatory. Access is limited to 49 visitors at any one time, so at the parking-lot gate you receive a ticket stamped with a "go time." In July and August expect a wait. You can picnic at one of the tables overlooking the river and explore the fort.

Fort Knox (fortknox.maineguide.com) tours are available Memorial Day–Labor Day, then weekends. In the visitors center interpretative panels tell the story: Built in 1844 of granite cut from nearby Mount Waldo, the fort includes barracks, storehouses, a labyrinth of passageways, and picnic facilities. The fort was to be a defense against Canada during the Aroostook War with New Brunswick. It's a venue for reenactments and a wide variety of events, sponsored by Friends of Fort Knox.

Project Puffin Visitor Center (207-596-5566; projectpuffin.org; 311 Main St., Rockland) makes learning about Maine Audubon and National Audubon's partnership to reintroduce the puffin to Maine islands fun for children, who can crawl into a burrow and watch videos of puffins feeding their young in their own burrows.

Lighthouse lovers will stop at the Maine Lighthouse Museum (207-594-3301; mainelighthousemuseum.com; 1 Park Dr., Rockland) to see the largest collection of lighthouse Fresnel lenses on display in the United States along with other lighthouse parts that were superseded by the automation of lighthouses. One-hundred-plus lighthouse keepers since the 1830s were women, one exhibit explains.

The Maine Lobster Festival, the first weekend in August, crowds the town with visitors who feast on 20,000 pounds of lobsters at the public landing and worship a sea goddess.

Down one of the two long peninsulas that run south is The Olsen House (207-596-6457; Hawthorn Point Rd., Cushing), open seasonally and owned by Farnsworth Art Museum. It's familiar from *Christina's World* and many of Andrew Wyeth's famous paintings.

The artist has no monopoly on the beauty of the landscape, of course. On the peninsula farther east, a drive down Rt. 131 south from Thomaston brings you around many inlets and views out to sea until your arrival at Port Clyde. The ferry

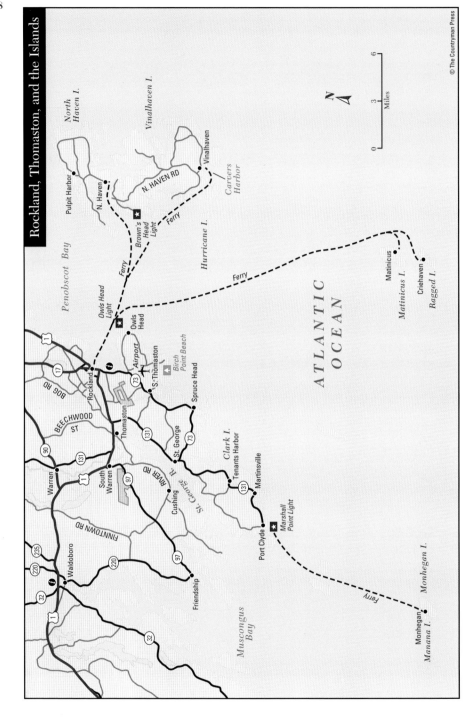

Rockland, Thomaston, and the Islands

© The Countryman Press

Robert Indiana at the Farnsworth

Nancy English

for Monhegan (see below) leaves from the dock, but if you can't jump aboard, a meal of seafood on the wharf at The Port Clyde General Store is an amiable way to enjoy the waterfront. And you might glimpse artist Jamie Wyeth on his way out to the family island enclave.

Just down the street from the village, the Marshall Point Lighthouse Museum (207-372-6450; marshall point.org; Marshall Point Rd., Port Clyde) presents the history of the town of St. George.

Returning to Rockland via Rt. 73, you can enjoy boiled lobster at Miller's Lobster Company (207-594-7406; millerslobsters.com; Spruce Head) or Waterman's Beach Lobster (207-594-7819; watermansbeachlobster.com; off Rt. 73, South Thomaston). BYOB and count on freshly baked pies.

Owls Head Transportation Museum (207-594-4418; owlshead.org; off Rt. 73 in Owls Head) keeps things interesting roundabouts year-round with special events—likely the swarm of antique cars that just passed you is heading there for

Marshall Point Lighthouse, Port Clyde

Nancy English

Waterman's Beach Lobster, South Thomaston   Nancy English

the rally. A ride in a Model T Ford is always on offer, and antique airplane shows and an "aerobatic airshow" might be just what you want to schedule a visit around. The Owls Head Light State Park nearby features a white, conical lighthouse built on a cliff in 1825.

A vineyard has added wine tastings to the area's offerings. Twenty-five hundred grapevines are planted at Breakwater Vineyards (207-594-1721; breakwater vineyards.com; 35 Ash Point Dr., Owls Head). It's open on weekends in summer and fall, presenting tastings of wine made with grapes grown elsewhere until the planted vines start to bear fruit.

Georges River Land Trust (207-594-5166; grlt.org; 8 N. Main St., Rockland) is based in Rockland, but its work involves land that stretches through the whole territory in this chapter. Protecting a 225-square-mile watershed, the trust provides public access to many of its properties. The Georges Highland Path covers 40 miles in four main sections, and a map can be found at the local chambers of commerce. Cross-country skiing is one possibility on a 7.2-mile section of the trail that passes Oyster River Bog; one access point is on Rt. 90 in Rockland, and another is on Beechwood St. in Thomaston.

Checking In

Best places to stay in Rockland and Waldoboro

Blue Skye Farm (207-832-0800; blue skyefarm.com; 1708 Friendship Rd., Rt. 220, Waldoboro) is a favorite spot of co-author Chris Tree. Original woodwork and fireplaces are part of the charm of a 1775 house restored with care by British innkeepers Peter and Jan Davidson. One hundred acres offer gardens for relaxation, trails for hiking, and a pond for skating. Guests can use the kitchen to make their own dinners or arrange a lobster dinner prepared by the hosts.

Berry Manor Inn (207-596-7696; berrymanorinn.com; 81 Talbot Ave., Rockland) is a luxurious retreat with canopy beds and whirlpool tubs, a deeply upholstered double chaise longue to drift off on in front of a wood-burning fireplace in Room 1, and a cathedral ceiling with Palladian windows in Carriage House Room 10. National Pie Day, January 23, is a local celebration that benefits the local food pantry. Pies both sweet and savory are to be had here and at the next three inns on that day, and maybe another if you ask nicely.

Granite Inn (207-594-9036; old graniteinn.com; 546 Main St., Rockland) holds gracious, handsome rooms with modern touches in its Federal Colonial house built of gray granite, which in 1984 was converted to an inn. The two front, second-floor bedrooms have a view of the harbor and the ferry terminal, and a family of four fits perfectly in the suite composed of Rooms 8 and 9. The breakfast baked goods are made from scratch.

The Captain Lindsey House (207-596-7950; lindseyhouse.com; 5 Lindsey St., Rockland) is run by Ellen and Ken Barnes, both previously captains of *Stephen Taber* and now enjoying the solid earth in this 1835 sea captain's house with nine rooms. Likely a fireplace and certainly a down comforter, big bathroom, and more will indulge you on your stay, when morning will bring a big English breakfast. Guests 55 and older might want to consider the special packages likely to be on offer.

LimeRock Inn (207-594-3762; limerockinn.com; 96 Limerock St., Rockland), a blue turreted Victorian, offers a wide porch with wicker furniture ready for relaxation. A room called North Haven has a cherry sleigh bed, and like every room is fully provided with toiletries and necessities. Whichever room you choose, the shops and restaurants are nearby, as they are for all these Rockland inns.

On Board a Windjammer

From late May to early October, the Windjammer fleet of Rockland and Camden provides cruises off the coast, and its popularity has remained strong ever since 1935 when artist Frank Swift transformed a few former fishing schooners into pleasure boats for tours of the islands. His inspiration that visitors would love to sail in comfort has always proved true. The **Maine Windjammer Association** (800-807-WIND; sailmainecoast.com) represents 12 Maine Windjammers, 7 of which are National Landmarks, and each is staffed with experienced, licensed personnel. Count on good food, six hours of sailing a day, and relaxation that will revive your love of life.

Stephen Taber (207-594-0035; stephentaber.com), for example, was launched in 1871. Twenty-two people can enjoy a cruise on this large sailing ship, the oldest U.S. sailing ship in continuous use. Captain Noah and Jane Barnes, the son and daughter-in-law of mother-and-father captains who first restored the ship, maintain the ship's reputation for fine dining, with culinary graduate and chef Aimee LePage in charge of the galley in 2010.

Three- to six-day cruises cost $400–1,100 per person and include all meals.

Local Flavors

The taste of Rockland—local restaurants, cafés, and more

Primo (207-596-0770; primorestaurant .com; 2 S. Main St., Rt. 73, Rockland) is the first (seasonal) destination for food lovers visiting from other part of Maine and the rest of the world. Chef Melissa Kelly owns Primo with pastry chef Price Kushner, and together they create dinners you will remember with pleasure, from the glass of exceptional wine to the house-cured prosciutto, guanciale, and more, made from the business's own Tamworth pigs. On the hill behind the restaurant in its restored Victorian house are gardens burgeoning with tomatoes, lettuces, cauliflower, fava beans, cardoons, squash plants, and far more. Ravioli with herbs, kale, pancetta, and an egg yolk with brown butter Pecorino sauce features it all.

Lily Bistro (207-594-4141; lily bistromaine.com; 421 Main St., Rockland) opened in 2008 and gave the town yet another reason to rejoice in its fine dining. Chefs Lynette Mosher and Robert Krajewski show off their love for fine food in menus stuffed with pierogi, steak frites, pork with spaetzle, and halibut with chorizo and clams. Brioche and crème fraîche tart comes with strawberries and toasted almond ice cream.

Conte's (148 S. Main St., Rockland) is high on the list because it's an experience, and possibly one you will hate. That keeps it lively at dinner—when you should be forewarned that you cannot pay with credit cards, you cannot phone or make reservations, and you order from a menu at the door and dine atop newspapers. Huge portions, and an attitude. But folks who like to eat leftovers for days will feel appreciative.

Café Miranda (207-594-2034; cafemiranda.com; 15 Oak St., Rockland) needs reservations, because the

Shopping in and Around Rockland

Rockland shops to visit are too numerous to mention, but we can't omit the bookshop/coffee shop **Rock City Books and Coffee** (207-594-4123; 328 Main St.), an oasis of caffeine and verbiage. New and used books accompany the iced coffee or toasted bagels with cream cheese like tires need roads and fish need water. Next door is **The Black Parrot** with fine clothes, housewares, and more—visit the back room to find deals. Down Rt. 1, back in Thomaston, is the **Maine State Prison Showroom** (207-354-9237). The prison has moved but the showroom remains, selling wooden furniture and small items made by prisoners.

On Rt. 1 between Thomaston and Rockland is the local landmark, **Dorman's Dream,** a perfect place to stop for an ice cream cone.

Dorman's Dream near Rockland
Nancy English

endless possibilities on the menu are too intriguing to forget and the locals return over and over again. Friendly and fun, the staff have a jovial quality surely as a result of the boisterous owner Kerry Altiero. At least, he seems boisterous because of that relentless menu. Try the Maine shrimp and mussels in Thai red curry coconut broth.

Suzuki's Sushi Bar (207-596-7447; suzukisushi.com; 419 Main St., Rockland) serves the best sushi on the Midcoast and likely Down East. The owner sources her seafood and shellfish from the freshest possible markets and her own and her staff's fishing expeditions: Mushimono donburi—steamed dishes—include salmon ponzu, and Maine shrimp with bonito dashi silver sauce. Noodle bowls might hold local oysters

with daikon and scallions in a kelp dashi broth. You will rarely have been fed this well.

Amalfi on the Water (207-596-0012; amalfionthewater.com; Ocean St., Rockland) moved to its new location from Main St. with a loyal following happy to enjoy the kefta anywhere. Oysters on the half shell, shrimp with garlic and fried calamari take inspiration with the view of the water, and bouillabaisse, paella, and moussaka show the range in the kitchen.

Rustica (207-594-0015; 315 Main St., Rockland) is a perfect place for a small or light meal or an herb-roasted chicken dinner. The Italian specialties are competent and the room is comfortable and relaxing. The eggplant Parmesan makes an excellent lunch.

Camden and Lincolnville

Check out these great attractions and activities . . .

Camden and Rockport both enjoy gorgeous harbors, and just inland from that pretty coast are the Camden Hills, 6,500 acres of which are wrapped up in Camden Hills State Park (207-236-3109; 280 Belfast Rd., Rt. 1), with hiking trails, camping sites, and a shore picnic area. Maiden Cliff Trail offers views from on top of 800-foot cliffs across Lake Megunticook, and connects with the Ridge Trail to the top of Mount Megunticook, the highest point on the Midcoast. Merryspring Nature Center (207-236-2239; merryspring.org; just south of the village off Rt. 1) is open year-round with walking trails and herb, daylily, and demonstration gardens. The Beech Hill Preserve (207-236-7091; coastalmountains.org; Beech Hill Rd., Rockport) is a prime spot for birding and for blueberrying, though you can't pick the berries unless it's one of the annual free picking days. The berry harvest is sold to support the preserve.

The towns, inhabited year-round by writers, retired intelligence officers, and plain old wealthy people, have art, crafts, galleries, and concerts galore, and even the Great Recession has not, so far, made a difference in that rich array. The Center for Maine Contemporary Art (207-236-2875; cmcanow.org; 162 Russell Ave., Rockport) had a blow in the fall of 2009 but recovered with a new director and direction. Exhibitions are offered into the early winter. Other galleries, just a few of many fine ones in the area, include Prism Glass Gallery on Rt. 1 in Rockport and Carver Hill Gallery, 264 Meadow St. in Rockport, with painting sculpture, fine crafts, and handmade furniture. Maine Media Workshops (207-236-8581; theworkshops.com; Rockport) draw students of photography, filmmaking, and more to Rockport every summer for one of more than 200 programs for every skill

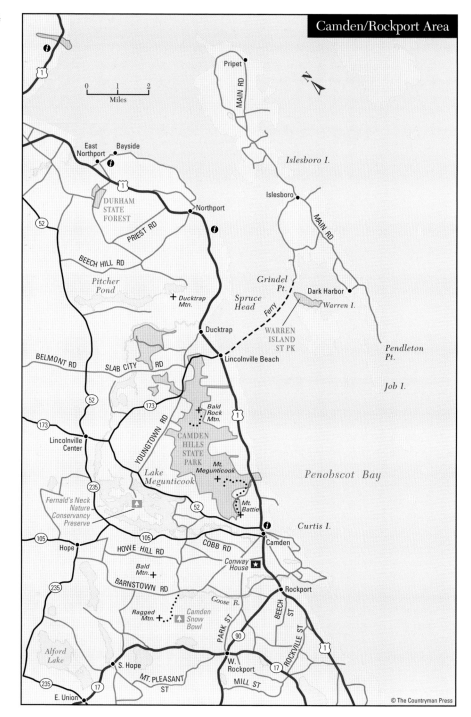

Camden/Rockport Area

Pripet

MAIN RD

Islesboro I.

East Northport
Bayside

DURHAM STATE FOREST

Northport

Islesboro

MAIN RD

PRIEST RD

BEECH HILL RD

Pitcher Pond

Ducktrap Mtn.

Spruce Head

Grindel Pt.

Ferry

Dark Harbor

Warren I.

Ducktrap

WARREN ISLAND ST PK

Pendleton Pt.

BELMONT RD

SLAB CITY RD

Lincolnville Beach

Job I.

Bald Rock Mtn.

CAMDEN HILLS STATE PARK

YOUNGTOWN RD

Lincolnville Center

Lake Megunticook

Mt. Megunticook

Penobscot Bay

Fernald's Neck Nature Conservancy Preserve

Mt. Battie

Curtis I.

Hope

HOWE HILL RD

COBB RD

Camden

Bald Mtn.

Conway House

BARNSTOWN RD

Rockport

Goose R.

BEECH ST

Ragged Mtn.

Camden Snow Bowl

Alford Lake

PARK ST

90

ROCKVILLE ST

S. Hope

W. Rockport

17

E. Union

MT. PLEASANT ST

MILL ST

0   1   2
Miles

© The Countryman Press

Camden Amphitheater

Nancy English

level. The Center for Furniture Craftsmanship (207-594-5611; woodschool.com; 25 Mill St., Rockport) offers another kind of class, with hands-on workshops for novice, intermediate, and advanced woodworkers. The Messler Gallery on the campus of the center shows off some of the finest examples of wood craftsmanship during five annual exhibitions.

Just behind the busy sidewalks of Camden is a lovely park beside its harbor, and between that park and the handsome library is a tranquil, shaded amphitheater.

Windsor Chairmakers (207-789-5188; windsorchair.com; Rt. 1, Lincolnville Beach) produces Windsor chairs and much more, with tours offered of the workshop.

The Owl and Turtle Book Shop (207-236-4769; 32 Washington St., Camden) and Sherman's Books (207-236-2223; shermans.com; 14 Main St., Camden) feed a population hungry for reading matter.

Bay Chamber Concerts (207-236-2823; baychamberconcerts.org; 58 Bay View St., Camden) presents concerts through fall, winter, and spring and sponsors a music festival in summer. Wednesday-evening summer concerts are in the restored Strand Theater in Rockland; on Thursday evening chamber music concerts are held in the Rockport Opera House.

Cellardoor Vineyard (207-763-4478; mainewine.com; 367 Youngtown Rd., Lincolnville) and Cellardoor Winery at the Villa (Rts. 90 and 1, Rockport) both offer free wine tastings. A replanting of the vineyard with grape hybrids suitable to the Maine climate means the wines being made until 2012 will comprise purchased grapes, but the owners are thrilled to be undertaking the revamping and revitalizing of this ambitious business.

In Northport, Swan's Island Blankets (207-338-9691; swansisland blankets.com; 231 Atlantic Hwy., Rt. 1) is looking for well-heeled customers, but everyone will wish to own one of these exquisite, handwoven blankets.

Past Lincolnville Beach is Belfast, a place with a wonderful downtown and a remarkable vitality. It's an annual destination just to taste the meals at Chase's Daily (see below), a vegetarian restaurant that sells its own farm's produce. Galleries in Belfast like Roots & Tendrils (207-338-5225; rootsand tendrils.com; 2 Cross St.) show off a scrappy art culture happy to sell a 50-cent button from a gumball machine, as well as tree trunk faces sculpted by Ron Cowan. Waterfall Arts (207-338-2222; waterfallarts.org; 256 High St., Belfast) has both classes and exhibits.

Cellardoor Winery at the Villa, Rockport
Nancy English

Checking In

Best places to stay
in Camden and Lincolnville

Hawthorne Inn (207-236-8842; camdenhawthorn.com; 9 High St., Camden) has been carefully restored and added on to by owner Maryanne Shanahan. Her comfortable, handsome rooms hold the best amenities, and her breakfast features house hazelnut granola. The Camden Maine Stay (207-236-9636; camdenmainestay.com; 22 High St.) is just down the street, and holds the same kind of well-cared-for, handsome rooms furnished with taste and kept to a high polish.

A Little Dream (207-236-8742; littledream.com; 60 High St., Camden) farther up Rt. 1 and with comfortable chairs and bed, enjoys some water views from the hillside it sits on, so

Roots & Tendrils, Belfast   Nancy English

High Tide Inn, Camden

Nancy English

that the annual Parade of Sails can be enjoyed from a few rooms. Treetops has a private deck and the view is especially lovely when the full moon rises over Camden harbor.

Cedarholm Garden Bay Inn (207-236-3886; cedarholm.com; Rt. 1, Lincolnville Beach) offers a water view and private waterside cabins, so away-from-it-all you'll wonder if you just drive here from crowded Camden. An incredible garden is the first symptom of the lavish care at this spot with four perfect, upscale cabins or cottages, two set right on the sea.

Inn at Ocean's Edge (207-236-0945; innatoceansedge.com; Lincolnville Beach) is a modern hotel with two buildings, and the one called Hilltop holds rooms with balconies. The Spa building has two luxury suites and a vanishing horizon pool. The fine-dining restaurant here, The Edge, provides another reason to stay, and it also offers casual meals in a pub and outside on an oceanside patio. Sunday night is pizza night.

The High Tide Inn (207-236-3724; hightideinn.com; 505 Belfast Rd.,

Rt. 1, Camden), with ocean views and its own 250-foot private beach a short drive from Camden, holds a variety of accommodations that start below $100 even in high season. The fine knack for hospitality of its innkeeper Jo Freilich shows in the delectable popovers and muffins she serves her guests in the screened porch of the main inn. Motel rooms with connecting rooms work for families at the top of the property. Within hearing of the waves lower on the hill are commodious rooms with ocean views and big comfortable beds, while some of the charming cabins and three of the inn rooms look out at the vast sweep of the water of Penobscot Bay.

Local Flavors

The taste of Camden and Lincolnville—local restaurants, cafés, and more

Francine Bistro (207-230-0083; francinebistro.com; 55 Chestnut St., Camden). *Flavor* is the byword here, from dry-aged steak that tastes better than any beef you've ever had to incredibly fresh fish. Count on straightforward meals that are somehow better than seem possible, plus crusty fresh bread and good wine. The owner opened Shepherd's Pie (207-236-8500; 18 Main St., Rockport) in 2010. Chicken liver toast, fresh oysters, shepherd's pie made with lamb shoulder braised with Madeira, organic hamburgers, barbecued ribs—you read the menu item and you want it, it's that simple. One reason for the attraction is owner Brian Hill's years of finding out the best food sources in Maine, while sustaining the high reputation of Francine Bistro.

Paolina's Way (207-230-0555; paolinasway.com; 10 Bayview Landing, Camden) serves pizza with shrimp or pesto or mushrooms, as well as house lasagna and ravioli, and its own gelato. White Lion Raw Bar & Bistro (207-230-7102; 20 Bay View St., Camden) makes sure to have three varieties of oysters on hand, but its entrées of fish and its steaks are quite good, too. Halibut with coconut milk rice is one of the chef's inventions, inspired by the

Produce from Beth's Farm Market, Warren, is served at Francine Bistro, Camden.   Nancy English

Thai cuisine he has come to know well after friendship with a Thai family and his marriage to a Thai woman.

Whale's Tooth Pub (207-789-5200; 2531 Atlantic Hwy., Rt. 1, Lincolnville) presents the sea from outside and inside tables, serving battered fried fish and seafood Mornay. Huge logs are burned in the fireplace when the weather is cold, and the local brew from Andrew's Brewery is on tap.

Belfast and Searsport

Attractions, activities, accommodations, eateries, etc.

Penobscot Marine Museum (207-548-2529; penosbscotmarinemuseum.org; 5 Church St., Searsport) holds a fantastic archive of historical photographs, many on display. Our recent visit also included "Images of Childhood in Maine and at Sea" in the Fowler-True-Ross House, one of more than 10 buildings making up the museum campus; far more photos are available online after hours of volunteer labor spent scanning the collection. View ships' models and marine fine art, attend history conferences—one in the fall of 2010 about the sardine industry featured a sardine cook-off—and brace yourself against the raging storm winds of historic wealth and historic ruin on the Maine shipbuilding coast.

Fortunately life is quieter now in Searsport, with most of the shipbuilding consisting of putting together model kits at BlueJacket Shipcrafters (207-548-9974; bluejacketinc.com; 160 E. Main St., Searsport). Carriage House Inn (207-548-2167; carriagehouseinn.com; 120 E. Main St., Rt. 1) offers three attractive

Penobscot Marine Museum in Searsport
Courtesy of Penobscot Marine Museum

rooms in an 1874 house built by a sea captain—and visited by Ernest Hemingway, when it was owned by an artist friend.

Searsport is also well known for its flea markets, like The Hobby Horse Antiques Flea Market, on Rt. 1.

Just south in Belfast, The White House (207-338-1901; mainebb.com; 1 Church St.) is a stunning Greek Revival house listed on National Register of Historic Places. The Belfast Bay guest room is a study in raspberry and golden-brown wood, with a crystal chandelier in both the bedroom and the bathroom. Belfast Bay Inn (207-338-5600; belfastbayinn.com; 72 Main St.) is right in the middle of town, and its crystal chandeliers light up the lobby. The rooms are over the top with luxurious appointments, and some have a view of the harbor, a fireplace, and dining area; Room 303 has a rooftop deck.

Count on Belfast for good meals. Chase's Daily (207-338-0555; 96 Main St.) makes thin-crust pizza; soft corn tacos stuffed with black beans, spicy pepitas, feta, crema, and lime; and a huevos rancheros that made our day, its house ranchero sauce smoky and voluptuous. A side of steamed Swiss chard worked into the plate perfectly. Produce from Chase's Farm is sold in the back of the huge, high-ceilinged room. Call for hours.

Three Tides Waterfront Bar & Marshall Wharf Brewing Co. (207-338-1707; 3tides.com; 2 Pinchy Lane, Belfast) lies at the bottom of Main St. to the left, with a second-floor covered deck that overlooks the glittering blue water of Belfast Bay filled by the Passagassawakeag River. When you order the Pemaquid oysters on the half shell, you will be honoring ancient generations of residents of this area, from the indigenous members of the Wabenaki Nation to the early Europeans, who made oysters and clams joyful summer soul food. David and Sarah Carlson opened this place in 2003 and feature on tap some of the more-than-a-dozen brews made in their next-door craft brewery, Marshall Wharf Brewing.

Belfast street sculpture   Nancy English

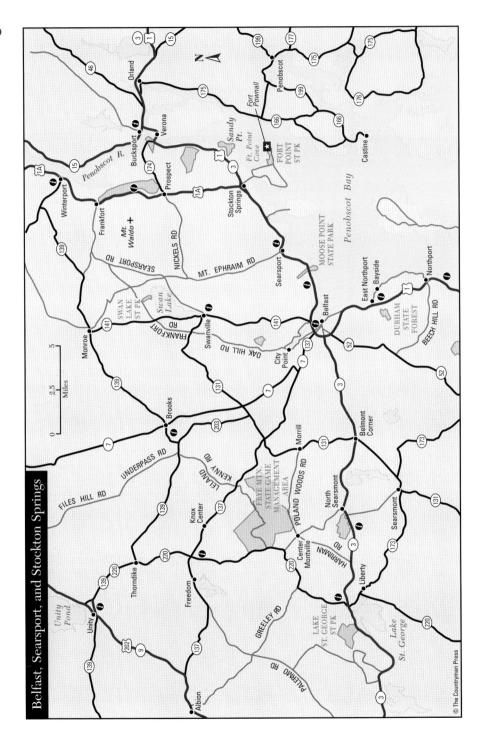

Belfast, Searsport, and Stockton Springs

© The Countryman Press

Hobby Horse Antiques Flea Market
Nancy English

Scoops & Crepes (207-338-3350; 35 Main St., Belfast) opened in June 2003 and has been lavishing Round Top ice cream, brownies, popovers, and both sweet and savory crêpes on its customers ever since.

Young's Lobster Pound (207-338-1160; 2 Fairview St., Belfast) sells cooked lobster and mussels, steamers, and lobster and crab rolls. The business is open year-round as a retail and wholesale seafood market, but takes off in the warm weather when its cavernous upper floor and a deck outside overlooking the water fill with hundreds of people ripping up their lobsters. Look no farther if you have a hankering for Maine's first citizen of the sea, but bring your own tablecloth and bottle of wine if you want to make this meal at all upscale.

Monhegan Island

Check out these great attractions and activities . . .

Spotting whales and porpoises on the hour-long ferry ride from Port Clyde or the hour-and-a-half ride from Boothbay Harbor or New Harbor, getting soaked in a downpour as you sit beside the ferry boat's stack—however you cross the miles of ocean to the island of Monhegan, you remember it. The journey breaks the hold of the mainland and ushers in another state of mind. Sitting still in the rocking *Linda B*, a World War II veteran that has shed her machine guns for freight, you have time to meditate on the swell of the cold salt water, the ups and downs without consequence, the rhythm of waves and days and calendars. By the time the boat curves right toward the island dock, sailing between the gray-shingled summer houses of the immaculate village and the stony green hulk of Manana Island, you've undergone a passage that's pressed out some of the kinks. You are ready to acknowledge happiness.

Three ferry companies can take you there. Monhegan Boat Line (207-372-8848; monheganboat.com) sails from Port Clyde, the *Balmy Days II* (207-633-2284; balmydaycruises.com) departs from Boothbay Harbor, and Hardy Boat Cruises (207-677-2026; hardyboat.com) offers trips from New Harbor that might include puffin sightings.

Early explorers like Captain John Smith and Samuel de Champlain arrived in the first years of the 1600s, and European fishermen, pirates, and others followed. Artists have sought out the island and its views, blind corners, and cottages since the middle of the 19th century, among them Rockwell Kent and Edward Hopper, who both painted landscapes of Blackhead cliffs on the northeastern end of the

Birding on Western Penobscot Bay

Birders book the Island Inn on Monhegan Island solid during the late-September and early-October migration season. Among the visitors are groups from Connecticut Audubon, WINGS—a Tucson-based birding tourism company that guides tours around the world—and the Manomet Center for Conservation Sciences, based on Cape Cod.

The charming island 12 miles off the coast of Maine, with its spectacular flocks of birds, as well as passing hawks and falcons, is just one of many places birds love to rest, breed, and winter in Maine. Western Penobscot Bay is rimmed with protected coastal wetlands along with the fine harbors that have given migrating birds refuge from time immemorial.

Belfast Harbor, for instance, holds 8 to 24 of the remaining 250 Barrow's goldeneye, a rare duck with yellow eyes set in its sleek, black-feathered head, from mid-December into March. With white markings and neck, the species attracts birders seeking rare sighting from around the world.

Maine Audubon and the Belfast Bay Watershed Coalition run a Bird Bus that operates in spring in Belfast. The Waldo County YMCA takes reservations and collects fees for the Tuesday trips from mid-March to early June.

"We look for returning waterfowl. My idea of the trips is to capture the progress of spring migration," said Seth Benz, who leads the tours. Benz, a Belfast resident and expert on birding, scouts for warblers up into the nesting season along with shorebirds, other songbirds, and raptors. In February, Benz hosts an event on the pedestrian bridge over Belfast Harbor to celebrate the flock of Barrow's goldeneye. In September he has taken the Bird Bus to Cadillac Mountain for the annual hawk watch. He also leads an Exploritas group, working with Elderhostel, in September to Monhegan.

Benz and mapmaker Margot Carpenter put together the *Belfast Important Birding Locations* brochure, available at the Belfast Chamber of Commerce.

Sears Island is one of the best places for birders during spring and fall migration, Benz said. In late fall and winter waterfowl frequent Fort Point Cove, Stockton Springs, accessible in and around the Fort Point Park. And at the mouth of the Ducktrap River near Lincolnville Beach in late autumn and winter, birders can encounter red-necked grebes, loons, mergansers, and several species of sea-ducks.

For fine birding places here and all over the Maine coast, *The Maine Birding Trail*, written by Bob Duchesne, is available at Maine Audubon in Gisland Farm, Falmouth, and online at Down East Books. You can download a free shorter brochure at mainebirdingtrail.com/Brochure.pdf.

island; three generations of the Wyeth family; and contemporary painter Sonya Sklaroff. Today paintings of the island are displayed in dozens of private studios and at The Lupine Gallery (207-594-8131; 41 Main St.) run by Jackie Boegel and Bill Boynton, who represent more than 60 artists. Private studios are open according to schedules posted on the Rope Shed on Main St. or on the outside of the studios you pass on your hikes. Artists stand at easels all over the island, and many rent shared houses for a week every year.

Monhegan is car-free, with only a few vehicles used for transporting supplies. Bikes are not allowed on the trails, and camping is not permitted. It's quiet and peaceful because 80 percent of the island is undeveloped. A total of 480 acres is maintained by the Monhegan Associates (monhegan assoicates.org), which publishes a hiking map detailing the island-wide trail system and its rules. No smoking is allowed outside the village in the extensive woods, and no outdoor fires are allowed. Given the island's inaccessible areas and the scarcity of water, fire is a constant danger to both the woods and the wooden houses.

Fish Beach, Monhegan   Nancy English

Trail walkers need to prepare themselves for poison ivy and ticks with long pants, for slippery rocks and rough ground with stout walking shoes, and for the likelihood of cold wind with a good windbreaker or fleece jacket. Swimming in the ocean is far too dangerous to attempt on the eastern side of the island, and kayaking undertaken only by experienced kayakers.

A first stop along the narrow roads that lace the village is at the Monhegan Island Light and its keepers' cottages. Here you'll find the Monhegan Historical & Cultural Museum (monheganmuseum.org; open 11:30–3:30 July–Aug., 1:30–3:30 June and Sept.). In 1824, when it was first built, the lighthouse burned sperm oil. Today the light is computer-operated by the U.S. Coast Guard with solar power. The Museum Association presents natural history artifacts upstairs; domestic and economic artifacts on the first floor in the Keeper's House; and annual art shows in the Assistant Keeper's House gallery.

Checking In

Best places to stay on Monhegan Island

To be sure of a room on your visit, as well as a parking place and a ferry ticket, make reservations. The Island Inn (207-594-8137; islandinnmonhegan .com) stands just above the ferry dock, a long, shingled summer hotel with a proper porch and lawn chairs overlooking the sunset and Manana Island. Old-fashioned and newly renovated, the comfortable dining room is hung with contemporary Monhegan paintings and serves exceptional and sophisticated dinners. A buffet breakfast comes with the rooms, which are divided between the main hotel and a rear annex. Request one with a view.

The Monhegan House (207-594-7983; monheganhouse.com) lies up the road. Its 28 rooms hold antique furniture and offer views of the sea and meadow. Most share the bathrooms on the second floor, but there are half-baths on the third floor and two suites with private baths. A full-service breakfast is included, but it's popular with the whole island so sometimes crowded. Single rooms on the fourth floor are bargain priced, usually reserved by artists. Dinner is served in high season; reservations are a must. The Trailing Yew (207-596-0440; trailingyew.com), on the road to Lobster Cove, invites you to "step back in time" in its guest rooms, many lighted by kerosene lamps. Scattered in several cottages and a main building, rooms share baths (with electricity). Rates include breakfast and dinner, where diners are seated at common tables and conversation abounds. No credit cards.

Shining Sails (207-596-0041; shiningsails.com), open year-round, offers the most comfortable accommodations on the island. The two rooms and five exceptional apartments are in a village home, most with decks and water

views. A continental breakfast is served seasonally in the living room by the woodstove. Hosts John and Winnie Murdock also offer nightly rentals elsewhere in village, along with some two dozen island cottages, available by the week.

Vinalhaven, North Haven, Matinicus, and Islesboro

Attractions, activities, accommodations, eateries, etc.

Both North Haven and Vinalhaven are reached by The Maine State Ferry Service (207-596-2202 in Rockland), with each island accessed by its own ferry. A day trip to Vinalhaven is possible if you leave early in the day, and we recommend a walk or bike ride to Lane's Island Preserve, with 40 acres of fields, beach, and marsh. But a longer stay is surely preferable.

The Vinalhaven Historical Society Museum (207-863-4410; vinalhavenhistoricalsociety.org; 41 High St.) is uphill from the ferry and worth the climb. The displays teach you the history of the island granite quarries, now fine swimming holes but originally the source for the gray stone used in buildings around New England. Fishing, island life, and the lobster industry are also described in exhibits. The Basin, a saltwater inlet, was once used to hold as many at 150,000 lobsters till the price peaked.

Tidewater Motel and Gathering Place (207-863-4618; 15 Main St., Carver's Harbor) has rooms that drink in the ocean air and views, with water racing close by and even underneath where the building spans a tidal stream. Decks on many of the 11

Eating Monhegan

Dinners at the **Island Inn**, **Monhegan House**, and the **Trailing Yew** are open to the public (all are BYOB). Wine, beer, and limited groceries are available at island stores, and the **Fish House Fish Market** is a source of fresh fish and seafood. The market is also the best place on-island for lobster rolls, crabmeat rolls, oysters, steamed clams, stews, and chowder, which patrons carry to picnic benches outside on Fish Beach for the best view on the island at sunset.

rooms in the motel, and accommodations in an adjacent building, offer you a choice. Bikes, car rentals, rides from the ferry dock, and more are part of innkeepers Phil and Elaine Crossman's day, as is good talk and fine writing— Phil Crossman wrote *Away Happens*, a book of humorous essays about island life. He and his wife also run Island Spirits (207-863-2192) with wine, cheese, beer, olives, and more.

Dinner at The Haven Restaurant (207-863-4969; 49 Main St.) is ambitious, with crabcakes and baked fresh scallops with crème fraîche, or roast pork tenderloin. A more casual pub-style menu is always available. At The Harbor Gawker (207-863-9365; Main St.) fried fish and lobster and crab rolls are the popular items.

Next it's time to visit The Paper Store (207-863-4826) to learn what's going on, and New Era Gallery (207-863-9351; Main St.) to drink in artwork by prominent Maine painters, sculptors, and photographers.

For a stay on North Haven, a room at Nebo Lodge (207-867-2007; nebolodge.com; 11 Mullins Lane) is just the ticket. Reopened after serving awhile as a private residence, this old inn has given the island a place to gather and given tourists a place to stay. Nine rooms, seven with shared baths, hold painted iron beds, wallpaper, and charm. Dinner will deepen the contentment, with rhubarb pie and cardamom ice cream on the menu one early summer night, and grilled leg of North Haven lamb or eggplant gratin available another night.

Coal Wharf Restaurant (207-867-2060; at the J. O. Brown & Sons Boatyard) is another option for local seafood and local produce.

North Haven Arts Enrichment Presentations, including plays and concerts, are performed at Waterman's Community Center in North Haven Village (207-867-2100; watermans.org). Artist Eric Hopkins has a gallery on North Haven (207-867-2229; erichopkins.com) that was a popular destination, at least until he opened another in Rockland at 21 Winter St. (207-594-1996). But North Haven Village also has North Haven Gift Shop and Gallery (207-867-4444)—which features changing exhibits as well as bags by well-known North Haven designer Angela Adams—and Calderwood Hall and North Island Fiber Shoppe (207-867-2265), offering paintings by Herbert Parsons, the owner, and hand-spun yarns from island sheep made by Mickey Bullock.

Visitors to Matinicus, 22 miles out at sea, must plan well to catch one of the four ferries that travel each month to the island. You might also climb aboard Captain George Tarkleson's narrated trip on the *Robin R* (207-691-9030; matinicusexcursions.com), or fly in with Penobscot Island Air (207-596-7500) from Owls Head Airport. Tuckanuck Lodge (207-366-3820; tuckanuck.com; Shag Hollow Rd.) provides a room and a kitchen to prepare lunch, serving dinner BYOB, year-round.

Visitors to Islesboro, reached by ferry from Lincolnville Beach, won't find anyplace to stay at all these days, so a visit is either a day trip or involves a rented cottage (islesboro.com/rentals). A car is almost a necessity on this long, rural island. Artisan Books and Bindery (207-734-6852; artisanbooksandbindery.com; 509 Pendleton Point Rd.) is a fine small bookstore with coffee and muffins served. A second location at 300 Main St. holds 20,000 volumes and is open summer afternoons. You can find ice cream and sandwiches at The Dark Harbor Shop (207-734-8878) in summer, but call first to make sure it's open.

6

Blue Hill and Deer Isle

The series of peninsulas and islands defining the eastern rim of Penobscot Bay, an intermingling of land and water along bays and tidal rivers, is a landscape that's exceptional, even in Maine. One finger of land, with Castine at its tip, points down along the Penobscot River toward the bay, but the bulk of the Blue Hill Peninsula wanders away southeast. It's divided from Deer Isle by the 10-mile-long Eggemoggin Reach, a busy shortcut between Penobscot and Jericho Bays. The reach is spanned by a vintage-1939, improbably narrow, soaring suspension bridge to Little Deer Isle, which in turn is a stepping-stone linked by a causeway to Deer Isle proper. Stonington at its southern tip is the departure point for Isle au Haut. Technically Stonington is just 36 miles south of Rt. 1, but the drive takes an hour and, if you stop in Blue Hill, as you must, and find your way to Brooklin or Brooksville, as you should, it can take several satisfying days.

The entire area is webbed with narrow roads threading numerous land fingers, leading to studios of local craftspeople and artists. What you remember afterward is the beauty of clouds over fields and quiet coves, some amazing things that have been woven, painted, or potted, and conversations with the people who created them.

Blue Hill Peninsula

Check out these great attractions and activities . . .

The first Rt. 1 turnoff for the Blue Hill Peninsula (bluehillpeninsula.org) is Rt. 175, the way to Rt. 166 and Castine (castine.me.us). Occupying a mini peninsula at the confluence of the Penobscot and Bagaduce Rivers, this town still looms larger on nautical than road maps and remains a popular yachting port. It is also home to the Maine Maritime Academy and its training vessel, *State of Maine*, which is open to visitors for tours mid-July–mid-Aug.

Castine is one of Maine's most photogenic towns, its streets lined with handsome 19th-century clapboard homes and buildings, all uncannily well preserved. Even the elm trees that arch high above its sloping Main St. escaped the general

147

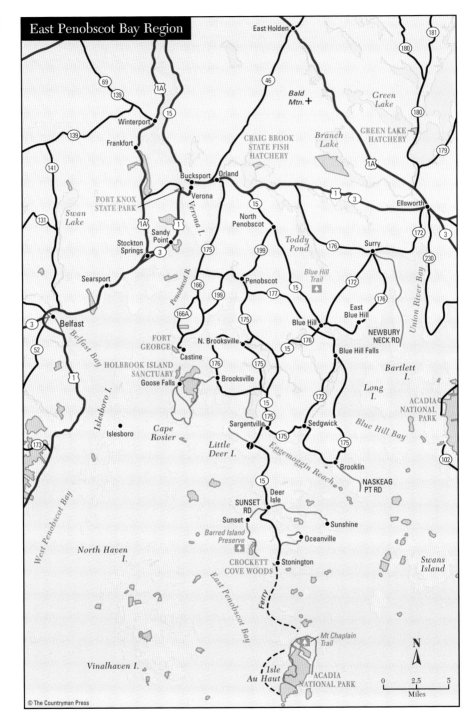

East Penobscot Bay Region

© The Countryman Press

State of Maine at the Castine Town Dock

Christina Tree

blight, and the post office is said to be the oldest continuously operating such facilitiy in the country. Most of the eight hotels built here during the steamboat era are gone, but descendants of the families who arrived by steam or sail still return each summer.

According to the historical markers that pepper its tranquil streets, this town has been claimed by four different countries since its early-17th-century founding as Fort Pentagoet. All of downtown Castine is on the National Register of Historic Places. Pick up the free pamphlet *A Walking Tour of Castine*, available at local shops. Begin at the town dock, with its welcoming picnic tables, parking, and restrooms. Amble uphill past antiques shops or down along Perkins St. to the Wilson Museum (207-326-8545; wilsonmuseum.org), with historical and changing art exhibits. The Castine Historical Society (207-326-4118; castinehistoricalsociety .org), housed in the Abbott School Building on the town common, is well worth a visit to see its multimedia presentation about the infamous defeat of the colonial navy here by the British during the Revolution (see *Sense of Place*). Up on Battle Ave. you can also inspect Fort George, the unimpressive earthenworks fortification the British built and then occupied during the War of 1812 as well as the Revolution.

Due to its relative isolation, Castine seems sleepier each summer while the town of Blue Hill seems busier. *Blue Hill*, we should clarify, here refers to a specific hill, a village, a town, a peninsula—and also to an unusual gathering of artists, musicians, and craftspeople.

Over the entrance of the Bagaduce Music Lending Library (207-
374-5454; bagaducemusic.org) on Rt.
172 in the village of Blue Hill, a mural
depicts the area as the center of con-
centric creative circles. Back-to-the-
earth pioneers Helen and Scott
Nearing, searching for a new place to
live "the Good Life" in the 1950s,
swung a dowsing pendulum over a
map of coastal Maine. It came to rest
on Cape Rosier, a mini peninsula pro-
truding westward. For many decades
the small town of Brooklin was a
familiar byline in *The New Yorker*
thanks to E. B. White, who also wrote
Charlotte's Web and *Stuart Little* here
at about the same time millions of children began to read about Blueberry

Main St., Blue Hill   Christina Tree

Hill in Robert McCloskey's *Blueberries for Sal* and about Condon's Garage in
South Brooksville in his 1940s classic *One Morning in Maine*. Energy lines or not,
this peninsula is exceptionally beautiful, with views to the east across Blue Hill Bay
toward Mount Desert as well as back across Penobscot Bay.

A dozen miles south of Rt. 1 via Rt. 15, the town of Blue Hill (bluehillme
.gov) is cradled between its namesake
hill and bay. At the walkable center of
town you'll find a pillared town hall, a
handsome WPA library (207-374-5515;
5 Parker Rd.), and Federal-era historic
houses, like the Jonathan Fisher
House (jonathanfisherhouse.org). The
summer season here roughly coincides
with the Kneisel Hall Chamber Music
Festival (207-374-2811; kneisel.org),
one of the oldest chamber music festi-
vals in the country, with a series of
Sunday-afternoon and Friday concerts,
June–Aug.

Judith Leighton at The Leighton Gallery, Blue
Hill   Christina Tree

Blue Hill's shops and galleries
showcase the best of the peninsula's
artists and artisans, among others.
Handworks Gallery (207-374-5613;
handworksgallery.org; 48 Main St.) is
filled with stunning handwoven clothing, jewelry, furniture, rugs, blown glass,
and art. North Country Textiles (207-
374-2715; northcountrytextiles.com),
corner of Main and Union streets,

Handworks Gallery, Blue Hill   Christina Tree

specializes in custom rag rugs, pottery, handcrafted woodwork, and woven clothing. The Jud Hartmann Gallery (207-374-9917; judhartmanngallery.com; 79 Main St.) exhibits Hartmann's nationally known realistic bronze sculptures of northeastern Native Americans as well as the work of other prominent local artists, like Randy Eckard (207-374-2510; randyeckard paintings.com). Eckard's own gallery is at 29 Pleasant St. across from Blue Hill Books (207-374-5632; bluehill books.com), a long-established, independent, full-service bookstore with frequent author readings. Be sure to stop by the Leighton Gallery (207-374-5001; leightongallery.com; 24 Parker Rd.), one of Maine's oldest and most prominent contemporary art galleries, with exhibits on three floors and an extensive sculpture garden. Owner Judith Leighton's own oils alone are worth a stop. At the northern end of town on Rt. 172, Rackliffe Pottery (207-2297; rackliffepottery.com) produces distinctive small pieces, featuring local clays and their own glazes. Visitors are welcome to watch. Pick up a copy of the free *Arts Guide*, available in most shops and galleries, highlighting studios throughout the peninsula.

There is no single best way to continue south from the town of Blue Hill. Whichever road you choose, you strike gold but miss another sterling route. The most direct road to Deer Isle is Rt. 15, which runs down the center of the peninsula. If you follow this route, we suggest that you detour the short way on Rt. 176 to South Brooksville. Buck's Harbor Market at its center offers a lunch counter and good picnic fixings; across the way is sheltered Buck's Harbor with its vintage yacht club. Hikers and birders continue north from the village and then left onto Cape Rosier Rd., forking onto Back Rd. to Holbrook Island Sanctuary State Park. A bridge across fast-moving, reversing Goose Falls leads to

Good Life Center, Cape Rosier   Christina Tree

the tiny village of Harborside. Continue south along the shore to find Good Life Center (207-326-8211; goodlife.org), Helen and Scott Nearing's Forest Farm, now open to the public in July and Aug. Back on Rt. 15 be sure to stop before the bridge at the pull-out on Caterpillar Hill, where there's a spectacular panorama west across Penobscot Bay to Camden Hills. This is a popular spot at sunset.

Another way south from Blue Hill takes you along Blue Hill Bay to Brooklin. It begins with Rt. 172; then at 2.5 miles, turn left onto Rt. 175 and head over the bridge across reversing Blue Hill Falls, a favorite spot with kayakers pitting their skill against the white water. Continue 9.5 miles south along the bay to the Brooklin general store and down Naskeag Rd. to the WoodenBoat School (207-359-4651; woodenboat.com). A spinoff from *WoodenBoat* magazine, this nationally famous seafaring institute offers courses that range from building your own sailboat or kayak to navigation. The store is a shopping destination in its own right. From Brooklin, Rt. 175 shadows Eggemoggin Reach, joining Rt. 15 just north of the Deer Island Bridge.

Checking In

Best places to stay on the Blue Hill Peninsula

Blue Hill Inn (207-374-2844; blue hillinn.com; 40 Union St., Blue Hill), a classic 1830s inn on a quiet village street, offers comfortable elegance in 11 guest rooms, two with kitchen facilities in the neighboring Cape House cottage that's open year-round. Guests gather in the parlor or garden in the evening, and rates include a full breakfast, served in a large, sunny dining room. North of the village of Blue Hill on Rt. 15, Blue Hill Farm (207-374-5126; blue hillfarminn.com; 578 Pleasant St.) is less formal and moderately priced. Here a former barn has been reworked as an open-beamed combination breakfast/dining/living room. The seven upstairs guest rooms are small but comfortable; the attached farmhouse offers seven more guest rooms with shared baths. Rates include a generous continental breakfast.

In Castine the Pentagoet Inn (207-326-8616; pentagoet.com; 26 Main St.) is a lovingly restored, turreted Queen Anne–style survivor from the steamboat era. Guest rooms in the inn itself are unusually shaped, and all 16 (including the neighboring annex) are imaginatively furnished with comfortable antiques. Innkeeper Jack Burke presides in the exotically decorated Passports Pub, an inviting gathering sport, along with the wicker-furnished and flowery veranda.

Pentagoet Inn, Castine   Christina Tree

The dining room is ranked among Maine's best. Up at the end of Battle Ave., The Manor Inn (207-326-4861; manor-inn.com) also has plenty of appeal. Open year-round, this expansive 1890s stone-and-shingle summer mansion is set above lawns in 5 acres bordering conservation land. The 14 rooms vary (as do the rates) from huge to snug, but each has its appeal. Guests can participate in morning Iyengar yoga classes offered by innkeeper Nancy Watson. In Penobscot, on the way to Castine, the Brass Fox Bed and Breakfast (207-326-0575; brassfox.com; 907 Southern Bay Rd.) is a 19th-century farmhouse filled with antiques. It offers ample common space, the second-floor guest rooms share balconies with views across fields and woods, and breakfasts are a point of pride.

The remaining best places to stay on the peninsula are widely scattered. The Surry Inn (207-667-5091; surry inn.com) is on Rt. 172 between Blue Hill and Ellsworth, not a bad location for exploring Mount Desert as well as this peninsula. Longtime innkeepers Peter and Annelise Krinsky offer eight moderately priced, old-fashioned, spanking-clean rooms, many with water views, with lawns sloping to Contention Cove, ideal for launching and paddling a kayak. The Surry is also a great spot for dinner. The Brooklin Inn (207-359-2777; brooklininn.com; 22 Reach Rd.) is a casual, friendly, year-round haven also best known as a restaurant. The four moderately priced, pleasant upstairs bedrooms cater to yachtsmen (innkeeper Chip Angell picks up at nearby moorings).

On Cape Rosier, well off the beaten track, Hiram Blake Camp (207-326-4951; hiramblake.com) has been operated by the same family since 1916, explaining the great value as well

The Surry Inn, between Blue Hill and Ellsworth   William A. Davis

as peace this family-geared compound offers. This is the kind of place where you come to stay put. All cottages (5 one-bedroom, 6 two-room, 3 three-bedroom) are within 200 feet of the shore, with views of Penobscot Bay. Each has a living room with a wood-burning stove; some have a fireplace as well. In shoulder seasons guests cook for themselves, but in July and August everyone gathers for breakfast and dinner in the dining room—which doubles as a library, because thousands of books are filed away by category in shelves ingeniously hung from the ceiling. Many guests bring kayaks, and there are rowboats at the dock.

Cottage Rentals
Peninsula Property Rentals (207-374-2428; peninsulapropertyrentals.com), Main St., Blue Hill, features a range of area rentals. Also see Maine Vacation Rentals (207-374-2444; mainevacation rentalsonline.com), 105 Main St., Blue Hill.

Two former full-service resorts offer cottages in superb settings. Oakland House (207-359-8521; 435 Herrick Rd.) in Brooksville offers 10 one- and two-room cottages scattered through the woods and along the shorefront, which includes a beach, at the entrance of Eggemoggin Reach. Its exquisite site property can only come from being in the same family since 1889. The same goes for the seven cottages at The Lookout (207-359-2188; thelookoutinn.biz; 455 Flye Point Rd.) in Brooklin. Here the extensive property faces across Blue Hill Bay toward Mount Desert. The seriously old-fashioned old hotel functions primarily as a restaurant. It's a popular place for weddings.

Local Flavors

The taste of the Blue Hill Peninsula—local restaurants, cafés, and more

Arborvine (207-374-2119; arbor vine.com), Main St. (Rt. 172), just south Blue Hill Village, is one of the most widely acclaimed restaurants in Maine; dinner reservations may be necessary a couple of days in advance. Chef-owner John Hikade and his wife, Beth, restored this handsome 1820s Hinckley homestead, retaining its original Dutchman's pipe vine above the door. The several open-beamed dining rooms with fireplaces, once the parlors, are simple and elegant. The menu presents local produce in memorable ways, maybe Bagaduce River oysters on the half shell with a frozen sake mignotte, or broiled Stonington halibut with grilled polenta, lemon butter crumb crust, and orange-miso sauce. The restaurant's piano bar, The Vinery

(no reservations), features wine by the glass and light bistro fare.

Table, A Farmhouse Bistro (207-374-5677; 66 Main St., Blue Hill) is the prime middle-of-town lunch and dining spot. It's changed hands and names over the years and at present features locally sourced comfort foods including pizzas and homemade pâté and sausages; for $24.50 there's lobster macaroni and cheese. The preferred dinner dining is downstairs along an enclosed porch, above a rushing stream. At lunch and all afternoon there's café seating outside and inside on the ground level; a bistro menu is offered all afternoon and evening.

Elsewhere on the peninsula Buck's Restaurant (207-326-8688) is hidden in the middle of South Brooksville, behind the Buck's Harbor Market. Chef-owner Johnathan Chase has an enthusiastic following, and his informal dining room, decorated with work by local sculptors and artists, is known for turning local ingredients into memorable meals. The Brooklin Inn (see *Places to Stay*), open year-round, religiously serves only wild fish and produce that's local and organic; the menu changes nightly. The setting is a pleasant dining room and sunporch in this venerable village inn. Elsewhere in Brooklin, The Lookout Inn & Restaurant (see *Places to Stay*) is a bit of a local secret, with consistently good dining on a many-windowed sunporch overlooking meadows that slope to the bay.

At the opposite end of the peninsula, 5 miles south of Rt. 1, the Surry Inn (again, see *Places to Stay*) is another local dining secret, offering exceptional value and views over Contention Cove. Chef-owner Peter Krinsky is known for signature dishes like lobster meat served with freshly shucked corn bound with a scallop mousseline.

In Castine the Pentagoet Inn (see *Places to Stay*) is a seasonal dining destination for many miles around, thanks to current CIA-trained chef Gina Melita. Signature dishes include Stonington crabcakes and lobster bouillabaisse. Dine in an airy, candlelit dining room with well-spaced tables, on the porch, or in Passports Pub.

At The Manor Inn (see *Places to Stay*), open year-round, co-owner Nancy Watson is the chef and the crabcakes are a family recipe. In addition to the formal dining room overlooking a sweep lawn, the appealing Pine Cone Pub here offers a lighter menu. For casual lunch or dinner in Castine, Dennett's Wharf (207-326-9045), near the town dock, occupies an open-framed harborside structure said to have been built as a bowling alley after the Civil War. It features homebrew and a huge all-day menu. When the summer sun shines, The Breeze is also a great place for fried clams and soft ice cream, right on the town dock.

If you're looking for a quick bite in Blue Hill there are several local secrets.

Kathleen McCloskey's Blue Hill Hearth (207-610-9090; 58 Main St.) bakes artisan breads (focaccia is a specialty), serves pizza, and makes terrific sandwiches in a small space with limited seating behind North Light Books (limited indoor seating, more outdoors). The Fish Net (207-374-5240) at the southern end of the village on Rt. 15 (across from the Rt. 176 turnoff) serves the best lobster and crab rolls in town; its picnic tables are also a good spot to feast on lobster and steamers (there's inside seating as well). Bird Watcher's Store & Café (207-374-3740; birdwatchersstoreand cafe.com; 37 Water St.) is also a good spot for salads and frittatas. South of town Barncastle (207-374-2300; 125

South St.) on Rt. 172/175 offers a sleek setting for wood-fired pizza, lunch through dinner. Marlintini's Grill (207-374-2500) south on Rt. 15/176 is a combination sports bar and family restaurant, open for lunch and dinner.

If it's a sunny day, a steady stream of traffic heads south on Rt. 15, then turns onto Rt. 176 north and follows it west a mile or to Bagaduce Lunch (open daily 11–7, closing at 3 on Wed.), a family-owned takeout since 1946. Here the fishburgers are enormous, crispy-fried fresh fillets and the clam baskets are legendary. Tables are scattered on waterside slope with the coveted seats by Bagaduce Falls, a prime spot to watch swift-moving reversing tides and the seabirds that feed there.

Blue Hill's Big Event of the year is The Blue Hill Fair (immortalized in *Charlotte's Web*), celebrated all Labor Day weekend, culminating with fireworks best viewed from the top of nearby Blue Hill (as in *Blueberries for Sal*).

Bagaduce Lunch, South Penobscot

Christina Tree

Deer Isle, Stonington, and Isle au Haut

Check out these great
attractions and activities . . .

Deer Isle is characterized by the kind of coves and lupine-fringed inlets equated with "the real Maine." It's divided between the towns of Deer Isle and Stonington, and there are vestiges of onetime communities like Sunset southwest of the small but very real village of Deer Isle and Sunshine, home to the nationally respected Haystack Mountain School of Crafts. Galleries display outstanding work by dozens of artists and craftspeople who live, or at least summer, in town.

The village of Stonington at the southern tip of the island remains a working fishing harbor, home to one of Maine's largest fishing/lobstering fleets. Most of its buildings, scattered on smooth rocks around the harbor, date from the 1880s to the World War I boom years, during which Deer Isle's pink granite was shipped off to face buildings such as Rockefeller Center and Boston's Museum of Fine Arts. There's still one small working quarry here on Crotch Island. The Deer Isle Granite Museum (207-367-6331; Main St.) depicts Stonington at the height of the granite boom with a population of 5,000; the present combined year-round population of Deer Isle and Stonington is 2,400.

The summer season is short but busy, with a number of seasonal shops and galleries along waterside Main St. However, the Opera House (207-367-2788; operahouse.org) stages live presentations and films year-round, and core restaurants and places tend to remain open. While property values have soared in recent

Eggemoggin Reach Bridge

Christina Tree

years, the number of nature preserves has multiplied, including many maintained by the Island Heritage Trust (207-348-2455; island heritagetrust.org). Six miles offshore, the southern half of Isle au Haut is part of Acadia National Park (nps .gov/acad).

Crossing the 0.5-mile, soaring Deer Isle Bridge is an adventure in itself, especially on a foggy night when you seem suspended inside a cloud. Of all Maine's "hinged" islands, this is the only one with a bridge long and dramatic enough to reinforce your feel of leaving the mainland behind.

The seasonal, volunteer-staffed Information Building (with facilities), maintained by the Deer Isle–Stonington Chamber of Commerce (207-348-6124; deerisle.com), is just beyond. Even if it's closed you can usually pick up the chamber's current map/guide outside; if it's open be sure to snag leaflet guides to island walking trails. Nearby Scotts Landing, for instance, is a 24-acre preserve on Eggemoggin Reach that includes a sandy beach. There's also parking along the causeway to Deer Isle.

It's just 5 miles down Rt. 15 to Deer Isle Village, but half a dozen rewarding detours to studio/galleries beckon. Down Reach Rd., for instance, the Greene-Ziner Gallery (207-348-2601; melissagreene.com) is a barn, surrounded by meadows, filled with Eric Ziner's ornate and whimsical metal sculpture and Melissa Greene's thrown earthenware pieces. Be sure to stop just north of the village at the Turtle Gallery (207-348-9977; turtlegallery.com), showcasing exceptional jewelry as well as biweekly changing shows of contemporary crafts.

Deer Isle Village is sited at the island's narrow waist, with water on both sides of its short main street (Rt. 15A). Here Lester Gallery (207-348-2676; thelester galleryllc.com; 4 Main St.) features Terrell Lester's striking local "lightscapes"; Red Dot Gallery (207-348-2733; reddotgallery.net; 3 Main St.) is a cooperative showing the work of 10 established local artists in mixed media, painting, fiber, jewelry, and clay; and Deer Isle Artists Association (207-348-2330; deerisleartists.com; 15 Main St.) is a 150-member cooperative with frequently changing exhibits. Don't miss the Periwinkle, a tiny shop with a vintage-1910 cash register, crammed with books and carefully selected gifts and cards.

Rt. 15 snakes south to Stonington but, again, there are enticing detours. The Sunshine Rd. branches off and winds 7 miles to Haystack Mountain School of Crafts (207-348-2306; haystack-mtn.org). Studios are generally closed aside from a weekly tour and scheduled events, but the campus itself is a work of art, a series of spare, shingled buildings, all weathered the color of the surrounding rocks and fitted between trees, connected by steps and terraced decks, floated above lichens and wildflowers on land sloping steeply to Jericho Bay. Keep an eye out on the way to and from for studio/galleries. There's no missing Nervous Nellie's Jams and Jellies (207-348-6182; nervousnellies.com; 98 Sunshine Rd.) with its whimsical life-sized sculptures, including a red lobster playing checkers as a 7-foot alligator looks on. Tea, coffee, and scones are served here, along with wild blueberry preserves, blackberry-peach conserve, and hot tomato chutney.

Half a dozen miles farther down Rt. 15 the Oceanville Rd. presents another tempting detour. The big attraction here is defunct Settlement Quarry, now a trail-webbed nature preserve with a view off across Webb Cove. Not far beyond is Old Quarry Ocean Adventures (207-367-8977; oldquarry.com; 130 Settlement Rd.), the departure point for Captain Bill Baker's seasonal excursions to Isle au

Haut as well as a variety of other cruises. This is also the area's prime source for guided kayaking and kayak rentals. The waters off Stonington are studded with islands, ideal for kayakers. Old Quarry also offers platform tent sites and a camp store.

Stonington Co-op by Jill Hoy

The village of Stonington is the iconic Maine village. Its mansard-roofed houses are perched where rocks permit, and the harbor is filled by afternoon with fishing boats; for Wind-jammers this is a weekly port. The narrow main street is now home for a dozen or so seasonal art galleries, with receptions on first Fridays, July–Oct. (stoningtongalleries.com). At the east end of Main St., bold, bright landscapes by Jill Hoy (207-367-2368; jillhoy.com) are housed in a big white barn. The gWatson Gallery (207-367-2900; gwatsongallery.com; 68 Main St.) shows contemporary painting and sculpture featuring prominent East Coast artists, and Isolos Fine Art (207-367-2700; isolasfineart.com; 26 Main St.) is a cooperative showing painting, sculpture, photography, and mixed media art by more than a dozen local artists.

Among the special shops here, don't miss Dockside Books and Gifts (207-367-2652; 62 W. Main St.) at the far end of the village. Al Webber's waterside bookstore has an exceptional selection of Maine books and gifts, sweaters by local knitters, and a great harbor view from the deck. Virginia Burnett's landmark Prints & Reprints (207-367-5821; 31 Main St.) features framed arts and antiquarian books, and The Dry Dock (207-367-5528) at the center of Main St. stocks tempting women's clothing and crafts.

gWatson Gallery, Stonington   Christina Tree

The hilly island visible from downtown Stonington is Isle au Haut (pronounced *eye-la-HO*), named "high island" in 1605 by Samuel de Champlain. This is a substantial island, 6 miles long and 3 miles wide, home to some 80 year-round residents, including best-selling author Linda Green-law, who has depicted island life in *The Lobster Chronicles*. From Stonington the Isle au Haut Ferry Service (207-367-5193; isleauhaut.com) makes the 45-minute crossing frequently in-season, stopping twice daily in warmer months at Duck Harbor in the Acadia National Park section of the island. There are no reservations on the ferry, but those with camping reservations are given priority.

Dockside Books & Gifts, Stonington
Christina Tree

Most visitors come to hike the 20-mile network of trails around Dark Harbor and along the cliffy southern tip. On a beautiful day, though, it's enough of an excursion to take the ferry to the town dock and walk to The Sea Urchin (207-335-2021)—Jim and Martha Greenlaw's gift shop—and neighboring Black Dinah Chocolatiers (207-335-5010; blackdinahchocolatiers.com), a café with WiFi, featuring amazing fresh cream truffles and other chocolates made right here. Of course, to really enjoy the island without pressure of catching a boat, you need to spend a couple of days. Diana Santospago of the Inn at Isle au Haut (207-335-5141; innatisleauhaut.com) meets her guests at the boat and offers a packed lunch and bicycles as well as breakfast.

Checking In

Best places to stay in Deer Isle and Stonington

At the Inn on the Harbor (207-367-2420; innontheharbor.com; 45 Main St., Stonington; open year-round) guest rooms come with binoculars, the better to focus on lobster boats and regularly on the schooners in the Maine Windjammer fleet, for which each of the 14 comfortable rooms is named. The inn backs on Stonington's bustling Main St., but most rooms, some with decks, face the harbor. Our favorites are the *Stephen Taber* (a former barbershop), and the *American Eagle* suite with two bedrooms, an open kitchen, a dining area, and a living room. A flowery ground-floor deck is shared by all.

The gracious, four-story, hip-roofed Pilgrim's Inn (207-348-6615; pilgrimsinn.com; open mid-May–mid-Oct) stands in the middle of Deer Isle Village but both fronts and backs on water. Built as a private home in 1793, it has big front parlors and guest rooms of varying sizes, some with gas log fireplaces. There are also three nicely decorated, two-bedroom cottages. The inn's dining room, The Whale's Rib, is open by reservation to the public.

Deer Isle's other full-service lodging is Goose Cove Resort (207-348-2600; goosecovelodgemaine.com; 300 Goose Cove Rd.; open Memorial Day–Columbus Day) in Sunset, on the western side of the island. There are five rooms in the lodge, which is primarily a restaurant, serving three meals; 16 cottages are scattered through the 21-acre property, which adjoins the Barred Island Preserve, owned by The Nature Conservancy and beloved by hikers and birders.

Off by itself in a northern corner of Deer Isle, The Inn at Ferry Landing (207-348-7760; ferrylanding.com; 77 Old Ferry Rd.) overlooks Eggemoggin Reach. Open year-round, this 1840s seaside farmhouse offers water views, spacious rooms, and a common room with huge windows and two grand pianos. The six guest rooms include a master suite with a woodstove and skylights. There's also an adjacent two-story, two-bedroom, fully equipped housekeeping weekly rental.

In Stonington, Pres du Port (207-367-5007; presduport.com; W. Main and Highland Ave.) is a cheery, comfortable B&B in an 1849 home with a light- and flower-filled sunporch overlooking the harbor. Charlotte Casgrain is a warm hostess who enjoys speaking French and offers three imaginatively furnished guest rooms, one with a loft and kitchenette. The generous buffet breakfast—perhaps crustless crabmeat-and-Parmesan quiche—is served on the sunporch. Also in Stonington, Boyce's Motel (207-367-2421; boyces motel.com; 44 Main St.; open year-round) is a bit of a local secret, far larger than it looks from the street. Most of the 11, reasonably priced units, including several with cooking facilities, line a quiet lane that angles off from Main St.

The best selection of rentals on Deer Isle and Isle au Haut is through Island Vacation Rentals (207-367-5095; islandvacationrentals.biz), 50 Main St., Stonington).

View from Harbor Café, Stonington
Christina Tree

Local Flavors

The taste of Deer Isle and Stonington—local restaurants, cafés, and more

The Seasons of Stonington (207-367-2600; seasonsofstonington.com; 27 Main St.) occupies the prime dining spot on the harbor. It's open for all three meals but only Wed.–Sun. in high season, and otherwise weekends. Weather permitting, lunch and a "small plate" dinner menu are served on the deck; a fine-dining menu served in the attractive dining room stresses local ingredients.

In Deer Isle the Whale's Rib Tavern in Pilgrim's Inn (see *Places to Stay*) is housed in a many-windowed old barn with white-clothed tables. The frequently changing dinner menu might range from fish-and-chips to lobster and shrimp risotto. The Cockatoo Restaurant at Goose Cove (see *Places to Stay*) is open in season daily noon–9. Named for Suzen Carter's pet cockatoos, the dining room in this classic old lodge overlooks the water, and there's dining on the deck. The menu features the freshest of fish, also meat prepared in interesting ways by Azorean chefs. The house specialty is Portuguese paella.

On Rt. 15 between Deer Isle and Stonington, Lily's Café and wine bar (207-367-5936; 450 Airport Rd.) is an island favorite, with the best sandwiches, from veggie to Reubens, as well as salads, homemade soups, and fresh-baked breads; there are deli dinner to-go items. Hours are quirky: The café is open year-round for breakfast and lunch until 5 (3 in winter) but closed weekends, with breakfast until 10:30

but lunch all day, from 8 AM on; there's also a sit-down Friday-night dinner until 8 PM.

In the middle of Stonington the Harbor Café (207-367-5099) is a dependable oasis, open year-round from 6 AM until closing, spanking clean and friendly with booths, great for seafood every way from rolls to the all-you-can-eat Friday fish fry (reserve). Next to the quarryman statue on the dock there is also The Fisherman's Friend (207-367-2442; 5 Atlantic Ave.), open year-round for lunch and dinner. It's a vast barn of a place in which you can always find a seat, good for a wide choice of fried and broiled fish, chowders and stews, burgers, and more.

Acadia

INCLUDING MOUNT DESERT ISLAND AND ELLSWORTH

The lodestone of the Maine coast and likely of the whole state is Acadia National Park, the first national park east of the Mississippi River, which occupies almost half of the land of Mount Desert Island as well as other landmasses nearby. Hanging off the coast of Maine like an enormous lobster claw, Mount Desert Island or MDI is laced with lakes and almost cut up through the middle by Somes Sound, the closest thing to a fjord on the East Coast. The island's terrain is mountainous, and those mountains, so dramatic when seen by sea, are built of bare pink granite, the source of its name, bestowed by Samuel de Champlain in 1604, L'isle des Mont-deserts (pronounced with the accent on the second syllable).

Hudson River School artists who painted the Mount Desert landscape in the 1800s infused their signature numinous light into the surroundings—or was it vice versa? Bar Harbor was then called Eden and considered a paradise, at least in summer. Wealthy inhabitants of Mount Desert Island had arrived seeking the vision on the artists' canvases. They had built enormous "cottages" and grown to treasure their surroundings when other kinds of development pressures began to compete with the scenery by the end of the 19th century.

Luckily for their contemporaries and for the more than two million visitors who arrive annually today, the resources of those wealthy summer residents, including thousands of acres of land, were pooled into the first 11,000 acres accepted by the federal government as a park in 1919. Boston textile heir George Dorr began the campaign to amass acreage in 1901, finding a ready response among many, including Harvard University president Charles W. Eliot.

Appalled at the noisy invasion of early automobiles, John D. Rockefeller donated 45 miles of carriage roads and erected 17 stone bridges, each unique and elegantly arched over the crushed-stone roads now limited to bikes, walkers, cross-country skiers, and of course carriage rides and horses. But whether you visit Acadia by sitting inside a car touring the 27-mile Park Loop Road, or by climbing up the rungs of the iron ladders set into granite cliffs on the hardest trails, you will encounter its beauty many times over.

Nancy English

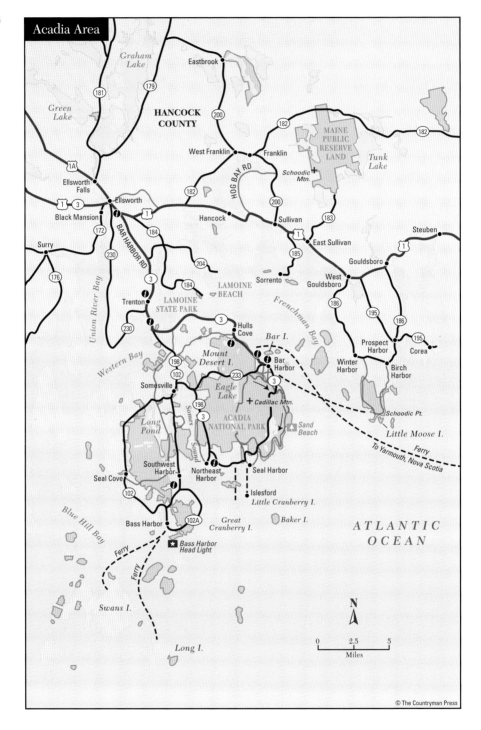

Acadia Area

Graham Lake

Eastbrook

181   179

Green Lake

HANCOCK COUNTY

200

182

MAINE PUBLIC RESERVE LAND

Tunk Lake

182

1A

Ellsworth Falls

West Franklin   Franklin

HOG BAY RD

Schoodic Mtn.

1   3   Ellsworth

182

200

Black Mansion   183

172   184   Hancock   Sullivan   East Sullivan

Steuben

Surry   230   1

185   Gouldsboro   1

176   204   Sorrento   West Gouldsboro

BAR HARBOR RD

3   184   LAMOINE BEACH   Frenchman Bay   186

Trenton   LAMOINE STATE PARK   195   186

230   3   Hulls Cove   Bar I.   Prospect Harbor   Corea

198   Mount Desert I.   Bar Harbor   Winter Harbor   Birch Harbor

Somesville   102   233   3

Eagle Lake   Cadillac Mtn.   Schoodic Pt.

198   Long Pond   ACADIA NATIONAL PARK   Sand Beach   Little Moose I.

3   Ferry

To Yarmouth, Nova Scotia

Southwest Harbor   Northeast Harbor   Seal Harbor

Seal Cove   102   Islesford

Little Cranberry I.

Bass Harbor   102A   Great Cranberry I.   Baker I.

ATLANTIC OCEAN

Ferry   Bass Harbor Head Light

Blue Hill Bay

Union River Bay   Western Bay   Somes Sound

Swans I.

N

Long I.

0   2.5   5
Miles

© The Countryman Press

Other sections of this chapter describes the towns and islands that surround the park, from Bar Harbor with its sidewalks crowded into the evening to Swan's Island, as peaceful as whatever weather is in charge. Most visitors travel here by car from Ellsworth down Rt. 3 past many quirky and engaging tourist businesses, but a meal in Cleonice, a visit to an elegant gallery in Ellsworth, and a devotedly French dinner at Le Domaine in Hancock are all excursions or detours more than worth your while.

Driving beyond Bar Harbor or bypassing its village entirely down the west side of the island brings you to many small, tranquil communities, some still infused by the traditions of wealthy summer visitors and others as quiet as any Maine town. Northeast Harbor and Southwest Harbor both contain fine shops, and at both towns' harbors you can embark on a ferry for the Cranberry Islands. Along the southwest edge of the island, in Bass Harbor, you can catch a ferry to Swan's Island and to Frenchboro's Long Island.

In 2009 you could still catch a ferry to Nova Scotia from Bar Harbor. Although that service was canceled in 2010, negotiations to resume ferry service were under way. Where the ferry might leave from, and even whether it will take passengers to Yarmouth, Nova Scotia—where ferries landed in the past—or scoot around the southern end to Halifax, is up in the air. The website novascotia.com, and any local chamber of commerce, could give you an update after this book goes to press.

Ellsworth and Hancock

Attractions, activities, accommodations, eateries, etc.

Ellsworth's brick-lined Main St. is part of Rt. 1 for a brief moment before you turn right onto Rts. 3 and 1, where travelers who opted to use the highway are heading south to MDI. But consider slowing to a stop in Ellsworth to enjoy art at the Courthouse Gallery (207-667-6611; courthousegallery.com; 6 Court St.), just up the hill from the stop sign south of Ellsworth village. The 1834 building is listed on the National Register of Historic Places and has been devotedly restored. Your eyes will be forgiven if they stray from the gleaming old floors and newly painted tin ceilings to the vibrant art on the walls. An affection for exuberant paintings and brilliant color mark the artwork exhibited here, like the moments revealed in John Neville's work, about dory fishermen off the coast of Nova Scotia, and Stephen Pace's galloping horses.

Around the corner from Courthouse Gallery, just down Rt. 172 in the direction of Surry, is Woodlawn Museum, Gardens and Park (207-667-8671; wood lawnmuseum.com; 19 Black House Dr.), where the Captain Black House museum is filled with 19th-century furniture (closed in winter), the gardens holds a tournament-sized croquet court for visitors to play on for a fee, and 2 miles of trails are open during daylight year-round. The Telephone Museum (207-667-9491; thetelephonemuseum.org; 166 Winkumpaugh Rd., off Rt. 1A north of Ellsworth) celebrates telephone technology with hands-on exhibits. Place a call to someone you know from a switchboard in the museum.

Kisma Preserve (207-667-3244; kismapreserve.org; Rt. 3, Trenton) is on the road to MDI, and you might pass it by thinking it's a hokey tourist trap. Instead, if you stop here you will encounter more than 60 species of animals who have found a home for retirement or after suffering injury or abuse, from a mountain lion to a moose, owls, turtles, and a white wolf, which adults can arrange to encounter up close. Rules are strict to maintain the tranquility that this preserve guarantees its animal residents.

The Grand Auditorium (207-667-9500; grandonline.org; Main St., Ellsworth) offers live performances and movies in its renovated and glorious interior. Much of Ellsworth was rebuilt during the worst of the Depression, a seeming miracle we could take some inspiration from.

A seasonal train ride from Ellsworth, Downeast Scenic Rail (207-667-7819; downeastscenicrail.org), brings riders into the countryside. Volunteers have devoted themselves to bringing this excursion into being, work well worth enjoying.

By now you're hungry. If it's lunch or dinnertime, your best bets are either Union River Lobster Pot (207-667-5077; lobsterpot.com; 9 South St.)—where you can enjoy a steamed lobster and all the fixings or superior fried seafood in a lovely setting on Union River (but call for hours)—or Cleonice (207-664-7554; cleonice .com; 112 Main St.).

Cleonice is open year-round with changing hours, and its offerings whet the appetite any time of year, with an emphasis on Mediterranean tapas, like terrific grilled baby octopus and delicate white anchovies, and finely prepared, wholesomely sourced ingredients including local grass-fed beef and fresh fish. Dinner entrées are big, small plates are an option, the wine list is good, and the restaurant, like something out of a noir film from the 1930s, feeds the hunger for adventure.

With all this going for it, Ellsworth is an option for an overnight stay made simple by the owners of Twilite Motel (207-667-8165; twilitemotel.com; Rt. 1), just south of the village. Inexpensive motel rooms, which are well maintained, come with a continental breakfast of muffins and coffee and with friendly owners who can guide your next steps on the coast. Small pets are welcome, for a fee.

Another calm spot on Rt. 1—a good base for forays to both Mount Desert Island and Schoodic Peninsula farther down east—is Le Domaine (207-422-3395; ledomaine.com; 1513 Rt. 1, Hancock), a luxuriously appointed inn with an excellent restaurant (and 10 percent off dinner if you stay here). A continental breakfast with croissants is served in the room. You won't go wrong with the Ris de Veau or sweetbreads, delicate and golden, duck confit, or roasted halibut for dinner, or with a bottle from the long French wine list. The more homey Crocker House Inn (207-422-6806; crockerhouse.com; Hancock Point) lies down the road to the old summer community of Hancock Point, and though it isn't on the water, the coast is a short walk away. Its 11 rooms are furnished with American antiques and quilts, with steak, duck with Grand Marnier ginger sauce, and scallops in lemon and wine sauce for dinner.

Campers looking for other sites than the often booked campgrounds on Mount Desert Island can enjoy an ocean view and beach at Lamoine State Park (207-667-4778; campwithme.com; Rt. 184).

Acadia National Park

Check out these great attractions
and activities . . .

First, of course, at the Hull's Cove Visitor Center, the park campgrounds, or the information center next to the Bar Harbor Town Green, pick up a week's pass ($20 with a car, $5 without) and receive a little introduction to the majestic sprawling realm of Acadia National Park (207-288-3338; nps.gov/acad; off Rt. 3 just north of Bar Harbor).

Most park get themselves to the top of Cadillac Mountain and around some or all of the Park Loop Road, most of it one-way. Built over the years between 1922 and the 1950s, with design insight from Frederick Law Olmsted Jr., the Park Loop Road offers good places to stop, hike, photograph, and contemplate the landscape of ocean, wood, and stone. The Island Explorer buses (207-667-5796; exploreacadia.com) are free, and its Number 4 Loop Road bus can take you around the sites, dropping off and picking up all day through Columbus Day. Stop at Wildwood Stables (877-276-3622; carriagesofacadia.com) and you can enjoy an hour carriage ride on the carriage roads for $18 (in 2010). If you are lucky enough to be able to bring your own horse, that horse can board at the stables ready for your daily rides, but there are no horse rentals.

Back on the bus, Number 3 Sand Beach takes passengers to Sand Beach and to Blackwoods Campground (207-288-3274; reservations required May–Oct. at 877-444-6777 or recreation.gov), one of two campgrounds in the park. The other is Seawall near Southwest Harbor, or a ride on Number 7—with sketchier service come fall.

From parking areas all over the island, most accessible by bus, the trailheads beckon. Precipice Trail featured iron rungs set into the nearly vertical route up

A marsh near Bass Harbor

Nancy English

Champlain Mountain, an attraction for the intrepid, but closed during peregrine falcon nesting. The Precipice Trailhead is on the Park Loop Road south of the Sieurs de Monts entrance off Rt. 3, south of Bar Harbor. Gentle, nearly horizontal Wonderland is a trail that stretches out over a point of land at the southern end of the island, off Rt. 102A between Seawall and Bass Harbor.

But altogether the park counts dozens of trails. Swimming, while forbidden on many of the lakes skirted by carriage roads, is offered at Echo Lake, with access off Rt. 102 south of Somesville and another little beach off Beech Mountain Rd. Sand Beach, off the Park Loop Road south of Bar Harbor, gives you the Maine ocean in its frigid glory, with water that stays 55 degrees and colder.

Just a little farther on the Park Loop Road is Thunder Hole, where the formation of the cliffs at the edge of the water amplifies the fury of the surf's roar—and where the allure of

Echo Lake   Nancy English

big surf proved fatal to several visitors in 2009. During Hurricane Earl's visit in 2010, park officials closed the area off entirely. Rt. 3 at Seal Harbor is often inundated with waves during big storms at high tide, and it's another good watch point for surf and waves.

Park rangers lead myriad activities at Acadia, and guest educators are another bonus. Birch-bark canoe and basket-making demonstrations from Passamaquoddy artist David Moses Bridges were free in 2010, for example, and ranger-led canoe trips, nature walks, and junior and senior ranger programs are offered all summer, with a monthly program schedule to be found at the park information centers.

During The Acadia Night Sky Festival (nightskyfestival.org), park employees show off the stargazing that Acadia, unpolluted with lights, presents every gaudy night of the year.

All season long, the fresh popovers at Jordan Pond House (207-276-3316; jordanpond.com; Park Loop Road near Seal Harbor) provide a respite on a tour of the park, whether by carriage, on foot, or by bicycle or car. With lawn seating overlooking the pond or indoor tables in a vast, handsome building, the restaurant, owned by the park, offers lunch, tea, dinner—and its specialty at all times, crisp, light, and airy popovers with butter and jam. Call for a reservation to assure your own.

So much of Bar Harbor burned during the Great Fire of 1947 that the village as it once stood can barely be imagined. Photographs of the Bar Harbor in its glory

Bar Harbor, Town Hill, and Hull's Cove

Check out these great attractions and activities . . .

can be viewed at the Bar Harbor Historical Society (207-288-0000; barharborhistoricalsociety.org; 33 Ledgelawn Ave.), where you can also learn more about the devastating conflagration.

The fire also mowed down stands of spruce and balsam firs that had ringed the town and clung to the bits of soil left among the granite outcroppings across the island, leaving hardwood seedlings with the chance to grow tall for the first time in, perhaps, centuries.

Today the logging that goes on maintains the woods instead of reaping them.

The birds are grateful. The Acadia Birding Festival (acadiabirdingfestival .com) of early to mid-June gathers guides and experts who offer tours, lectures, slide shows, and walks that could bring you up short near peregrine falcons or warblers on their summer visit to Maine. Michael B. Good (207-288-8128; downeast naturetours.com) leads Downeast Nature Tours throughout the year, with trips to special bird-watching sites like Three Pines Bird Sanctuary.

But during summer the main migrants to MDI are always found crowding the sidewalks of Bar Harbor, night and day. Shops, restaurants, and ice cream offer them diversions, but you get the impression that the vastness of the park might have driven them together after hikes and tours to take comfort from their own kind.

In any event, the July 4 Independence Day Celebration is thoroughly popular and includes music played on the town green and fireworks set off by the town pier a short walk away. The lobsters that race—or crawl, or dally, or retreat—down seawater-filled Plexiglas tracks at the athletic fields are the high point, with $1 bets adding to the drawn-out drama.

Inside Acadia National Park is the old Robert Abbe Museum at Sieurs de Monts Spring, accessible though the Wild Gardens of Acadia with more than 300 species of indigenous plants. Park founder George B. Dorr had his hand in this establishment, having bought up the natural spring to prevent its becoming a springwater business. But Dr. Robert Abbe was the genius of the original museum, building the structure in the late 1920s to protect his own and others' valuable collections of Native American artifacts. The temple-like building has a soul and poetry about it that appeal to any romantic of history—and when a door blew shut in 2001, we could have sworn Dr. Abbe himself had just taken his leave. The new branch of the Abbe (207-288-3519; abbemuseum.org; 26 Mount Desert St.) in downtown Bar Harbor present extensive collections acquired in the years since the museum's founding, including centuries-old basketry and crafts made by original inhabitants of Maine and the Maritimes from the Passamaquoddy, Maliseet, Penobscot, and Micmac Nations now collectively known as the Wabenaki.

The early-July Native American Festival and Basket Makers Market on the grounds of the College of the Atlantic gives visitors a chance to meet Wabenaki craftsmen and -women, listen to traditional music, and buy what is surely the best souvenir imaginable, a basket or other craft made with a history of tradition beyond memory.

And at the same place, The George B. Dorr Museum of Natural History (207-288-5395; coa.edu; Rt. 3, just north of Bar Harbor), with a tidal touch tank, brings you up close to wild animals and birds you might not otherwise get a chance to glimpse alive. At The Oceanarium (207-288-5005; theoceanarium.com; 1351 Rt. 3) the creatures under the waves are also at hand, with a marsh walk and lobster hatchery.

Of course, sometimes tourist traps are just the ($8.50 adult) ticket. Pirate's Cove, "The Original Adventure Golf," offers tee times nearly round the clock (well, 9 AM–10:00 PM) in-season. When you drive by, the spot's illuminated waterfalls and emerald putting greens appear like a vision out of the darkness. Watch out for the pirate's roar inside that cave!

Bar Harbor is a center for biking, with two big, full-service bike rental and sales shops and the wonderful Island Explorer Bicycle Express, a van with a bike trailer that chauffeurs bikers from the village green to the carriage road entrance of Acadia National Park on Eagle Lake. Avoid the roads this way and the biking is peaceful and serene. Kayakers can rely on the rental businesses themselves for a ride to a lake, and all of them offer guided kayaking tours. Sailors can find the *Margaret Todd* with her distinctive four masts and red sails on the waterfront at Bar Harbor, along with whale-watching ships and tour boats.

The Maine Crafts Guild Show (mainecraftsguild.org) in Bar Harbor in late August gets Martha Stewart's thumbs-up, with some of the best craftswork done in the state.

Checking In

Best places to stay
in Bar Harbor

Ullikana Bed & Breakfast (207-288-9552; ullikana.com; 16 The Field) has been our favorite bed & breakfast for years, and so long as innkeepers Helene Harton and her husband, Roy Kasindorf, stay at the helm, it will probably remain so. Their gracious hospitality sets you at ease from the get-go, and the stuffed baked pancakes at breakfast, on the lawn with the sea in the distance, are superb. Everything in the rooms is solid and well maintained, from the tiled floors to the exuberant decorative painting on the walls.

The Bass Cottage Inn (207-288-1234; basscottage.com; 14 The Field) is right next door, and has been decorated with elegance and style. Gas fireplaces, whirlpool tubs, and TVs are in all rooms, which are utterly comfortable, like the pillowtop beds. Count on a fine breakfast in the glassed-in porch and the friendly guidance of hosts Teri and Jeffrey Anderholm.

Somewhat less expensive, Primrose Inn (207-288-4031; primroseinn .com; 73 Mount Desert St.) has the same boon of great innkeepers, Catherine and Jeff Shaw, who have thought of everything—and responded to every request with improvements, like a generous breakfast and afternoon tea, perhaps with apple or blueberry pie.

The Saltair Inn (207-288-2882; thesaltairinn.com; 121 West St.) has a waterfront location in the historic district, three blocks from the middle of town. Suites and rooms offer gas fireplaces and some balconies overlooking the water.

Two big places for tourists who prefer them are Bar Harbor Inn (207-288-3351; barharborinn.com; Newport Dr.) and the recently built Harborside Hotel and Marina (207-288-5088; theharborsidehotel.com; 55 West St.).

Both perch over the harbor. Bar Harbor Inn is more old school, handsome and restrained, although new additions are fully outfitted and all rooms have what anyone would expect from a fine hotel. The Harborside is a little glitzier, and more expensive.

Local Flavors

The taste of Bar Harbor—local restaurants, cafés, and more

Burning Tree (207-288-9331; Rt. 3, Otter Creek) is at the top of its long-played game, serving fresh vegetables out of its own gardens and imaginative vegetarian and seafood dinners, like gray sole with sautéed radicchio and a Dijon cream sauce. Cantaloupe salad with chorizo was one special salad, and a purple basil mojito made a delicious cocktail.

Mache Bistro (207-288-0447; machebistro.com; 135 Cottage St.) was taken over by Kyle Yarborough in 2009, and his energetic presence gives the menu some pizzazz. The lobster cakes with cracked green olive relish were one pleasant surprise, and the bistro steak with Gorgonzola butter was just as good as you could wish. Pain perdu will tempt you beyond your capacity, so don't say you weren't warned.

McKay's Public House (207-288-2002; mckayspublichouse.com; 231 Main St.) was every single local's recommendation, and when we finally had a chance to find out why it became our own top choice in town. A good wine list and friendly atmosphere combine with excellence in the kitchen to make McKay's, open year-round, a favorite for the tourists, too. Grilled ocean perch with capers and brown butter accompanied by a glass of Cali-

fornia Fumé Blanc made one long drive a distant memory. Fish-and-chips, crabcakes, and roasted beet salad comprise the "elevated pub fare"—or just call it pub fare the way it should be, much of it sourced locally.

Café This Way (207-288-4483; cafethisway.com; 14½ Mount Desert St.) makes dinner, for which you should get a reservation, and breakfast, which can be equally crowded. The Ann, an omelet with goat cheese, basil, and tomatoes, hit the spot on a day when the big blueberry pancakes made someone's day at the next table. Dinner veers southwest with a shepherd's pie made with eggplant, spicy creamed corn, and onions; or off to Asia with Maine seafood spring rolls with plum sauce. Roast duck might come with spiced pears and blueberry "jus."

Reel Pizza Cinema (207-288-3811; reelpizza.net; 33 Kennebec Place) combines first-run movies with excellent pizza, all named for favorite movies. "Godzilla" is topped with sweet or hot sausage, pepperoni, onion, green pepper, mushroom, and tomato, while "Moonstruck" is all white, with ricotta,

Burning Tree   Matt McInnis

mozzarella, Parmesan, and Monterey Jack.

Sometime or other, either after the bike ride or following the movie, Mount Desert Island Ice Cream (207-460-5515; both 7 Firefly Lane and 325 Main St.) is a prime stop. President Obama thought so in 2010, when he opted for the coconut ice cream. Of course, a politician has to be cautious—the rest of us can go wild, with blueberry basil sorbet and salt caramel ice cream or anything else owner Linda Parker and her staff think up.

Northeast Harbor, Otter Creek, and Seal Cove

Attractions, activities, accommodations, eateries, etc.

Northeast Harbor lies across the mouth of Somes Sound from Southeast Harbor, and both small towns share a quiet tranquility far from the hustle of Bar Harbor, but Brooke Astor used to shop on the Main St.—and Martha Stewart still does. Inside Wikhegan Books (207-276-5079; 117 Main St., Northeast Harbor) you can find a copy of the Red Book, published annually, which lists summer residents and their winter addresses, new and old, along with advertising. "It's a social directory," said Richard Fuerst, who owns the bookstore with his wife. "It costs $8." Fuerst said Bar Harbor used to have a Blue Book, long gone, with similar social ambition.

Even if none of the Red Book names mean much to you, the shops show off expensive goods with a certain confidence that someone will come along with the wherewithal to buy them. Peter England sweaters for $495, thick, silky, and fabulous, fill a back table at The Kimball Shop & Boutique (207-276-3300; kimballshop.com; Main St., Northeast Harbor—kitchen and housewares are next door to the clothes shop). The rest of us need not fear—the basement room is stuffed with clothes on clearance and sale that are fabulous deals, if you don't mind that they are perhaps a season old, and make it easy to shrug off the sense that you're help being gifted with the cast-offs. Meanwhile, upstairs, a summer resident from Texas is selecting her entire year's wardrobe and having the staff pack it up to be shipped off.

Maine Coast Exchange (207-276-2008; 123 Main St., Northeast Harbor) might be working some local blues, too, as it accepts fine furniture, fashion, and jewelry on consignment. Look for the gorgeous driftwood from the Great Recession's outgoing tide here. Island Artisans (207-288-4214; 119 Main St., Northeast Harbor, and also at 99 Main St., Bar Harbor) sells fine crafts, including stunning basketry.

Instead of Bonwit Teller's—or was it Bendel's?—Bird's Nest Northeast Harbor has The Colonel's Restaurant & Bakery to retreat to for a cup of tea. The front seating area was empty one summer afternoon, perfect for that tea and a late-afternoon perusal of the New York Times.

Best of all would be to stay across the street in Maison Suisse Inn (207-276-5223; maisonsuisse.com; 144 Main St., Northeast Harbor), which provides a coupon for breakfast at the Colonel's with your choice of 10 light-filled, antiques-furnished rooms in a handsome old house wrapped in a garden.

The Asticou Inn (207-276-3344; asticou.com; Rt. 3, Northeast Harbor) might have been going through a transition year last year, when co-author Chris Tree

The Gardens of Mount Desert Island

The **Asticou Azalea Garden** and **Thuya Garden** (207-276-3727; gardenpreserve.org; both off Rt. 3 near its intersection with Rt. 198) are examples of the gardening ambition of Charles K. Savage, who in 1958 took advantage of two parcels of handsome real estate near his family's business, The Asticou Inn. His landscape architecture expertise helped to create two gardens as beautiful today as they have ever been in the past.

Sand Garden at Asticou Azalea
Nancy English

With the attention of the Mount Desert Land & Garden Preserve, an endowment created by the original owner of Thuya Lodge, Joseph Henry Curtis, who gave the lodge and its land to the island's residents, and the vision of Savage, Thuya Garden's trustee for 37 years, the gardens enjoy both the resources and the imagination formal landscape needs to inspire.

The Asticou Azalea Garden, with a small parking area off Rt. 198, must be lovely when rhododendrons and azaleas are blossoming, but its structure makes it splendid anytime, with a sand garden inspired by Japanese gardens and its raked crushed-stone path leading your steps from one elegant composition of trees, shrubs, and flowering plants to another.

Thuya Garden
Nancy English

Thuya Garden, which can be reached by a path of steps from Rt. 3 and which has a small parking lot up narrow Thuya Dr., is a long stretch of landscaped areas that you can view from the Upper Pavilion, an open shed with a long cushioned bench.

Many of the plants in both the wide, glamorous, Gertrude Jekyll–style perennial beds of Thuya Garden and the austere tapestry of the Azalea Garden come from Beatrix Farrand, a renowned gardener who had a garden called Reef Point in Bar Harbor that she uprooted and sold in 1956.

found it lacking. With a new general manager and owner, this year was looking up, the desk clerk said, and recent online reviews were uniformly favorable. With its beautiful location, heated pool, and multiple accommodations from a tiny single room to a house, the historic inn certainly has every physical thing going for it. Continental breakfast is included, and in good weather you'll enjoy it on the deck overlooking the harbor. Dinner at the Asticou's restaurant could start with

Damariscotta oysters wrapped in bacon and wind up with halibut and Himalayan red rice, or roasted Berkshire pork tenderloin.

Harbourside Inn (207-276-3272; harboursideinn.com; Rt. 198, Northeast Harbor) is a shingle-style "cottage" set on 4 acres. The trees obscure the harbor views, but the rooms have their own engaging pleasures, from fine 19th-century furniture, to fresh flowers, to the blueberry muffins served with breakfast on the sunporch.

Kimball Terrace Inn (207-276-3383; kimballterraceinn.com; 10 Huntington Rd., Northeast Harbor) is the place for inexpensive rooms with tennis and a pool—off-season deals are likely.

Asticou Inn   Nancy English

Southwest Harbor, Manset, and Bernard

Attractions, activities, accommodations, eateries, etc.

Ringing the southwestern coast of MDI, in a west-to-east direction, are Southwest Harbor, Manset, Bass Harbor, and Bernard, each with reasons to visit. Southwest Harbor is the largest community, and The Wendell Gilley Museum (207-244-7555; wendellgilleymuseum.org; Rt. 102) is one of its highlights. An amateur who became a master bird decoy carver, Gilley shaped more than 10,000 birds in his lifetime, beginning in the 1930s. Workshops in decoy carving could give you your own start at craftsmanship.

Another beacon of craftswork is inside Aylen & Son Fine Jewelers (207-244-7369; peteraylen.com; 332 Main St., Southwest Harbor), where Peter and Judy Aylen turn semiprecious and precious stones into exceptional jewelry.

The Claremont Hotel (207-244-5036; theclaremonthotel.com; 22 Claremont Rd., at the end of Clark Point Rd. in Southeast Harbor) is the oldest hotel on the island, but keen management sustains the beautiful accommodations, from inn rooms and suites to cottages. A great chef, Daniel Sweimler, has been keeping the kitchen skills high and dinner at The Xanthus beyond appetizing. In July and August lunch and cocktails are served at the Boathouse, on the water's edge. The croquet court lies below the porch and the dining room windows, ready for the Croquet Classic in August and all the hours of practicing that lead up to it. Clay tennis courts, bikes for tooling around the village, badminton, and a little beach are included in the rates, along with breakfast. You might want to pay for the rooms with a wonderful ocean view. A 15 percent gratuity is added to the bill.

Lindonwood Inn (207-244-3553; lindonwoodinn.com; 118 Clark Point Rd., Southwest Harbor) rents nine rooms year-round, and with a fire burning in the breakfast room the charm survives the cold. Some rooms have a fireplace of their own, and a balcony overlooking the water.

Red Sky (207-244-0476; redsky restaurant.com; 114 Clark Point Rd., Southwest Harbor) wins loyalty and praise year in and year out, for dinners of sole in brown butter, ground lamb with a cider mint reduction, and lobster risotto. A cheese course for dessert and a fine wine list make an evening here alluring.

And just down the road for another evening is XYZ Restaurant (207-244-5221; off Seawall Rd., Manset), where dinners are straight from Mexico. Familiar to the owners because they spend their winters there, Mexican food shows up on these Maine plates the way it was first imagined far

Claremont Hotel   Nancy English

south. Start out with the freshly squeezed lime juice drinks, either a margarita or a limeade, then dive into the colorful and tasty meals. Chilis rellenos—ancho chilis stuffed with corn and cheese—holds an almost meaty rich flavor. Count on a variety of chilis and tender pork and chicken dishes easy to love.

Beyond Bass Harbor and its ferry boats lies Bernard, where Thurston's Lobster Pound (207-244-7600; Steamboat Wharf Rd., Bernard) held the mantle of best MDI lobster pound for years. The jury is out nowadays, as management goes through changes; yet however humdrum the offerings, this remains one of the most scenic spots around, with a big deck situated on Bernard's working harbor.

Antique Wicker   Nancy English

On the way to the harbor you will see Linda Higgins's Antique Wicker store (207-244-3983; antiquewicker .com; 3 Wicker Way, Bernard), with 600 to 800 pieces of every school and style of wicker ever made, enough stock to furnish your own new oceanside cottage. The business has a second shop at 270 Main St., Southwest Harbor, and consolidation is being contemplated, so call first for hours and directions. Linda Fernandez Handknits (207-244-7224; next door to Antique Wicker in Bernard) sells sweaters, Christmas socks, and embroidered pillowcases.

Bernard

Nancy English

The Cranberry Islands

Attractions, activities,
accommodations, eateries, etc.

Reached by ferries and cruises that depart from both Northeast Harbor and Southwest Harbor, the Cranberry Islands make a fine day trip in the summer season. Little Cranberry, also known as Islesford, has the particular attraction of a wonderful restaurant open for lunch and dinner called The Islesford Dock Restaurant (207-244-7494; islesforddock.com). Cynthia and Dan Lief, owners, chefs, and managers, manage to stay smiling through the ebb and flow of crowds off tour boats, whose passengers clamor for the delicious burgers or maybe hanker after the daily mezze, an assortment of Middle Eastern dishes. Cantaloupe gazpacho with lobster and prosciutto is typical of the invention on the dinner menu, though do not worry if you'd rather have a plate of ribs or something else equally familiar and loved.

Longtime summer resident and potter Marian Baker is often at work at her shop, Islesford Pottery (207-244-5686), on the dock near the restaurant.

The Islesford Historical Museum (207-244-9224) is a private collection of artifacts now maintained by Acadia National Park. It offers intriguing seasonal exhibits.

Great Cranberry has a larger year-round population of lobstermen—perhaps 40 brave souls. With a general store for sandwiches, a historical society, and a café for meals and ice cream, the island is its own attractive destination away from it all.

Swan's Island and Frenchboro

Attractions, activities, accommodations, eateries, etc.

Island Cruises (207-244-5785; bass harborcruises.com; Little Island Marine, Bass Harbor) offers narrated trips including one to Frenchboro, with 50 year-rounders, on the lookout for birds and sea creatures. Captain Kim Strauss's family bought the Philip Moore House, where Ruth Moore, a well-known author, was born—it was a general store and boardinghouse, too. A lot of Ruth Moore's writings are about the comings and goings of people, Strauss said, and her take on summer people was a little bitter. "Islands are very different from the mainland. There's a tension on islands." Year-round island communities have mostly disappeared off the coast of Maine with the advent of railroads and the end of oceangoing schooners, and Strauss can tell you this history.

The Maine State Ferry (207-244-3254) serves Frenchboro's Long Island, with its seasonal dockside deli and Frenchboro Historical Society.

Also reached by that ferry from Bass Harbor, Swan's Island requires either a car of your own or indefatigable legs and a bicycle. The high point of the year for many of its inhabitants is The Sweet Chariot Festival (sweetchariotmusicfestival .com), when folksingers and performers gather on the island to sing chantey concerts in the afternoon, perform nightly concerts, and carouse at parties. Geoff Kaufman, Lisa Redfern and Randall Williams, Denny Williams, and VOCO, a three-woman group from Los Angeles, are just a few of the performers whose most distinctive moment came with the three-part harmony serenades of the schooners visiting just for this, sung from rowboats and kayaks in Burntcoat Harbor 4 miles from the ferry dock. Count on dancing, if not clogging, and impromptu music sessions. Carter House (207-266-0958 or 207-526-4198; swans-island-maine.us) is an inexpensive and appealing B&B run by Nancy Carter, who makes the reservations when you call Maine State Ferry (207-244-3254); she personally drove one guest all around the island for a tour. Carrying Place Market (207-526-4043; 40 North Rd.) serves takeout pizza, seafood, and sandwiches.

8

Way Down East

SCHOODIC TO EASTPORT, INCLUDING LUBEC, CAMPOBELLO ISLAND, AND EASTPORT

Schoodic

Check out these great attractions, activities, and eateries

Nowhere in Maine does the coast change as abruptly as along the eastern rim of Frenchman Bay. On the western side is Mount Desert Island with Bar Harbor and Acadia National Park, a magnet for everyone from everywhere. The northern and eastern shores are, in contrast, a quiet, curving stretch of coves, tidal bays, and peninsulas, all with views of Acadia's high, rounded mountains.

These views continue all the way down the western shore of the Gouldsboro Peninsula. The 2,100-acre headland at its tip, a land finger known as the Schoodic Peninsula (acadia-schoodic.org), is part of Acadia National Park (nps.gov/acad/planyourvisit/upload/schoodic.pdf). It's directly accessible late June–Aug. by ferry from Bar Harbor (207-288-2984; barharborferry.com), with connecting bus service to trailheads and points of interest via the Island Explorer (207-288-4573; exploreacadia.com).

This is one place along the coast, however, where we suggest land over water. The drive around the bay is so glorious that it's been nationally recognized as the 29-mile Schoodic Scenic Byway (byways.org/explore/byways/13792/index.html). It begins on Rt. 1 at the Hancock/Sullivan bridge and follows Rt. 186 down along the western shore of the Gouldsboro Peninsula, then loops around Schoodic.

From Sullivan the Schoodic Scenic Byway shadows the bay, offering spectacular views. The only detours we suggest here are for crafts studios, particularly thick right at the beginning, marked from the Sullivan Common. The Barter Family Gallery (207-422-3190; bartergallery.com), 2.5 miles down Taunton Bay Rd. from Rt. 1, is foremost among these. Philip Barter is nationally known for his bright, bold, and distinctive landscapes, sculpture, and furniture. The shop also features son Matthew Barber's paintings, wife Priscilla's braided rugs, family-made jewelry, and cards. On Rt. 1 itself be sure to stop at the scenic turnout just before Dunbar's Store for a spectacular view back across Frenchman's Bay.

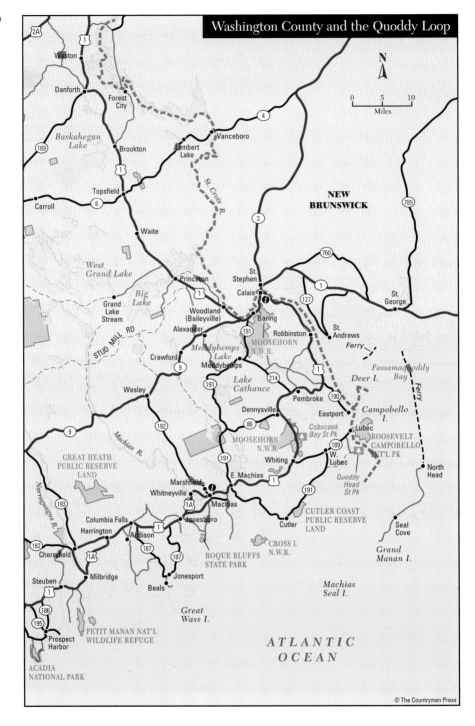

Washington County and the Quoddy Loop

View of Frenchman's Bay from a pullout on the Schoodic Scenic Byway   Christina Tree

Views continue as you follow Rt. 186 south to Winter Harbor at the entrance to the park. Until recently the village was home to a U.S. naval base that sent and intercepted coded messages from ships and submarines; it also serves a longtime summer community on neighboring Grindstone Neck. Check out the Winter Harbor 5 & 10 (winterharbor 5and10.com), chef-owned Fisherman's Inn Restaurant (207-963-5585; 7 Newman St.), and Chase's Restaurant (207-963-7171; 193 Main St), the local gathering place, open year-round for all three meals.

Barter Family Gallery in Sullivan   Christina Tree

The one-way, 12-mile shore road loops around Schoodic Peninsula; 7.2 miles of it are in the national park. Schoodic Point at the outer tip is a popular spot to watch surf in stormy weather. A mile or so farther along, the Blueberry Hill Parking Area accesses most of the area's hiking trails. Prospect Harbor at the eastern end of the park is a quiet fishing village from which Rt. 195 wanders off into the

Winter Harbor 5 & 10

Christina Tree

even quieter village of Corea. During the Schoodic Arts Festival (schoodicarts
.com), the first two weeks of August, this entire area comes alive with dozens of
arts and crafts workshops as well as performances. The festival underscores the
abundance of local talent; check acadia-schoodic.org for details about the many
studios and galleries. Back on Rt. 1 east, take the short signposted detour to
Bartlett Winery and Spirits of Maine (207-546-2408; bartlettwinery.com). Open
for tastings June–Oct., Tue.–Sat. 1–5, this is Maine's oldest winery, nationally recognized for its fruit wines and brandies.

Checking In

Best places to stay on the
Schoodic Peninsula

The Black Duck (207-963-2689; black
duck.com) in Corea is a fine old house,
steps from a picturesque working harbor. Barry Canner and Robert Travers
offer four guest rooms and ample common areas, all comfortably, imagina-
tively furnished with antiques and contemporary art, and two housekeeping
cottages right on the harbor. In Prospect Harbor, Elsa's Inn on the Harbor (207-
963-7571; elsasinn.com; 179 Main St.) is a gabled, mid-1800s family homestead
that Megan Moshier and her husband, Glenn, have totally renovated. The six
bright guest rooms with handmade quilts have water views, as do the spacious living room and veranda. Lobster bakes can be arranged for in-house guests. Oceanside Meadows Inn (207-963-5557; oceaninn.com) consists of an 1860s sea
captain's home and neighboring 1820s farmhouse overlooking Sand Cove.
Innkeepers Sonja Sundaram and Ben Walter are passionate conservationists, and
their 200-acre property is webbed with trails leading to a salt marsh; wildlife

About Washington County

Beyond Gouldsboro you enter Washington County, a ruggedly beautiful and lonely land unto itself. Its 700-mile coast harbors some of the most dramatic cliffs and deepest coves—certainly the highest tides—on the eastern U.S. seaboard, but relatively few tourists. Created in 1789 by order of the General Court of Massachusetts, Washington County is as large as the states of Delaware and Rhode Island combined. Yet it's home to less than 34,000 people, widely scattered among fishing villages, logging outposts, Native American reservations, and saltwater farms. Many people (not just some) survive here by raking blueberries in August, making balsam wreaths in winter, and lobstering, clamming, digging sea worms, harvesting sea cucumbers, and diving for sea urchins.

What happened along this particular coastline in prehistoric times has recently taken on new interest to scientists studying global warming. Apparently the ice sheet stalled here some 15,300 years ago, evidenced by the region's extensive barrens and number of bogs, eskers, and moraines. A free map/guide to 46 stops on *Maine's Ice Age Trail Down East* (iceagetrail.umaine.edu) is widely available.

The most recent development to affect travel to this area is, unfortunately, the requirement of passports or passport cards (see getyouhome.gov) to visit **Roosevelt Campobello International Park** (506-752-2922; fdr.net) just across the bridge from Lubec but technically in New Brunswick, Canada, from which it's separated by Passamaquoddy Bay.

We've divided our discussion of Washington County into two sections: *The Bold Coast*; and *Eastport, Cobscook, and Passamaquoddy Bays.*

includes moose and eagles. A rehabbed open-timbered barn is the venue for live performances and wedding receptions.

On Rt. 1 in Gouldsboro, Acadia View Bed & Breakfast (866-963-7457; acadia view.com) is a contemporary mansion designed and built specifically as a B&B, with guest rooms facing Frenchman Bay. Three miles south of Rt. 1, Bluff House Inn (207-963-7805; bluffinn.com) off Rt. 186 in South Gouldsboro is a modern lodge with reasonably priced rooms, including a two-room efficiency, and common space overlooking the water. The beach below is good for launching kayaks.

The Bold Coast: Milbridge to Lubec

Check out these great attractions and activities . . .

Washington County produces 90 percent of the nation's blueberries and is the world's largest source of wild, low-bush berries, the kind that grow best on the undulating "barrens" that you see as you continue to drive east. These literally turn blue by August when they're harvested, then red in the fall. As you enter Milbridge note the JASPER WYMAN AND SONS sign on a vintage, white-clapboard building, offices for one of the oldest and largest blueberry processors. Beyond Milbridge, Rt. 1 threads the blueberry barrens for much of the next 30 miles. Before setting off through this bleakly beautiful landscape, you might want to stop here at 44 Degrees North (207-546-4440; 44-degrees-north

.com; 17 Main St.), open year-round for lunch through dinner, good for affordable, digestible road food. The Milbridge Historical Society Museum (207-546-4471; millbridgehistorical society.org) has changing exhibits as well as displays on the town's vanished shipyards and canneries.

From Milbridge, Rt. 1A is the shortest way east, rejoining Rt. 1 in 8 miles. A few miles beyond, be sure to make the 0.25-mile detour into the village of Columbia Falls. At its center is the Ruggles House (207-483-4637; ruggleshouse.org; open June–mid-Oct., Mon.–Sat. for guided tours). This is a glorious Federal-style mansion built in 1818 with an exquisite flying staircase.

Ruggles House in Columbia Falls
Christina Tree

Next door at Columbia Falls Pottery (207-483-4075; columbiafallspottery.com; 150 Main St.) April Adams makes striking, useful pottery as well as custom Delft-style tiles.

The next worthwhile detour is Jonesport (jonesport.com) 12 miles down Rt. 187 from Rt. 1. It's a welcoming way stop facing Moosabec Reach, which is, in turn, spanned by a bridge leading to Beals Island. Both communities are all about fishing and together boast eastern Maine's largest lobstering fleet. The bridge is a viewing stand for the annual July 4 lobster-boat races, and Beals is known for the distinctive design of its lobster boats. You need to spend the night here to take advantage of local boat excursions or to hike Great Wass Island, a rugged hiking destination with 1,579 acres maintained by The Nature Conservancy; it's linked to the southern end of Beals. Heading back up from Jonesport on the eastern loop of Rt. 187, the Maine Coast Sardine History Museum (207-497-2962; 34 Mason Bay Rd.) is worth a stop.

April Adams of Columbia Falls Pottery
Christina Tree

Machias (207-255-4402; machias chamber.org), 20 miles northeast of Jonesport, is the seat of Washington County, also home to a branch of the University of Maine. A center of colonial resistance during the Revolution, it was repeatedly burned—but somehow the 1770s Burnham Tavern (207-255-6930; burnhamtavern.com) survived. It's just off Rt. 1 on Rt. 192, after you cross the bridge over Little Bad Falls. Downtown Machias comes alive during the Wild Blueberry Festival (third week of Aug.), but

Jonesport

Christina Tree

otherwise it's a far cry from its early-19th-century days as a major shipbuilding and lumber port. Most motorists stop here to fill their tank and their stomachs. Helen's Restaurant (207-255-8323), 11 Main St., on the water just before the causeway, is the county's best-known road-food stop. Big enough to gracefully accommodate buses, it also offers some gracious corners. Head for the far dining room and grab a booth by the water. The fish chowder is made daily with haddock, onions, Maine potatoes, butter, and cream, and the pies are legendary.

Helen's Restaurant, Machias

Christina Tree

East of Machias, Rt. 1 is a straight, heavily wooded road. It's 10 miles to Rt. 189 and another 11 to Lubec. Birders and hikers may want to turn off Rt. 1 in East Machias onto Rt. 191 to Cutler, departure point for Andrew Patterson's Bold Coast Charter Company (207-259-4484; boldcoast.com) tours to Machias Seal Island to see puffins (see the *Puffin-Watching* sidebar in *Basics*). Machias Seal is the only place you can actually view puffins on land; five-hour tours are offered, weather permitting, May–early Aug.

Captain Andy was the first to popularize the name *Bold Coast*, which is now used to promote a far larger area but originally applied just to the 20 miles of dramatically high cliffs between Cutler and West Quoddy Head. An extensive trail network along these cliffs is maintained by the Maine Bureau of Parks and Lands (207-287-4920; maine.gov/doc/parks); look for the CUTLER COAST UNIT TRAILS sign 4 miles east of town on Rt. 192. Other preserves maintained by the Quoddy Regional Land Trust (207-733-5509; qrlt.org) are spaced along the coast

Captain Andy of Bold Coast Charter Company heading for Machias Seal Island
Christina Tree

here. Rt. 191 turns inland at South Trescott to rejoin Rt. 1, but we usually continue along the coast on Boot Cove Rd. for another half a dozen miles through open barrens to Quoddy Head State Park (207-733-0911; maine.gov/doc/parks).

Despite its name, the red candy-striped **West Quoddy Head Light** marks the easternmost tip of the United States. There are benches for those who come to be among the first in the country to see the sunrise (fog permitting), and there's a beautiful 2-mile Coastal Trail along the cliffs to Carrying Place Cove. The **Keepers House** (207-733-2180; westquoddy.com) doubles as the area visitors center (open Memorial Day–mid-Oct.) and a museum, with displays that tell the story of the lighthouse, built in 1858.

Puffins on Machias Seal Island
Christina Tree

Lubec is half a dozen miles north of the lighthouse, linked by a short bridge to Campobello Island. Water St. here is transitioning from sardine cannery row to a lively lineup of shops and eateries. **McCurdy's Smokehouse** (207-733-2197; mccurdyssmoke house.org; 50 Water St.) here has been restored by Lubec Landmarks to evoke the era of smokehouses and canneries. For a taste of how good smoked fish can be, stop by the **Bold Coast Smokehouse** (888-733-0807; bold coastsmokehouse.com; 224 Country Rd., Rt. 189) on the edge of town.

An unlikely catalyst for the town's current upswing is **SummerKeys** (summerkeys.com), a series of weeklong programs for a variety of instruments, begun in 1992 and still orchestrated by piano teacher Bruce Potterton. With no prerequisite skills, students fill local lodging places, and there are weekly concerts in local venues. Hundreds of musicians have discovered Lubec this way and passed the word along about the town with a wandering, 97-mile coast, reasonably priced real estate, and an end-of-the-world feel.

From Lubec it's an easy walk across Roosevelt Campobello International Bridge into New Brunswick, but this was an easier stroll before recent passport requirements. Don't try it these days without a passport or a passport card; still, there's rarely more than a few-minutes wait at either inspection station. In summer, however, you lose an entire hour, given the fact that new Brunswick is on Atlantic Time, one hour ahead of Maine's Eastern Time.

If Campobello Island (campo bello.com) were in the United States—as it would be except for an 1840s treaty badly negotiated by Daniel Webster—it would undoubtedly be far

Hiking along the Bold Coast   Christina Tree

more crowded and less enjoyable. In 1881 much of the 9-mile-long island was sold to Boston and New York developers who built three large, now long-gone hotels. As happened from Kennebunkport to Bar Harbor, some wealthy families who patronized the hotels, the Roosevelts among them, built their own expansive summer "cottages." Franklin spent every summer here from 1883 (he was age one) until 1921, when he was stricken with polio.

The 2,800-acre Roosevelt Campobello International Park (877-851-6663; fdr.net; open daily, Memorial Day weekend–Columbus Day weekend), administered by a park commission composed of both Canadian and American members, was dedicated in 1964. The Visitors Centre here shows a 15-minute film dramatizing FDR's relationship to the island, and the exhibits focus not just on

West Quoddy Light   Christina Tree

Roosevelt but also on his times. The neighboring 34-room Roosevelt Cottage is sensitively maintained as the family left it, charged with the spirit of a dynamic man. Beyond this immediate compound the park includes 8 miles of trails and 15.4 miles of park drives, modified from the network of carriage drives that the wealthy "cottagers" maintained.

There's more to Campobello than the park. Follow Rt. 174 north for Herring Cove Provincial Park (506-752-2449) with its nine-hole golf course, restaurant, pebble beach, and 76 campsites, 40 with electrical hookups (reservations: 506-752-7010). The big attraction at the end of this road is the striking East Quoddy Head

Roosevelt Cottage, Campobello Island
Christina Tree

Lighthouse, known locally as Head Harbour Light. Built in 1829 and recently restored by a dedicated local group of "Friends," it is accessible only at low tide and with care; the tide surges in quickly through the narrow channel that separates it from the headland—where a small park offers a great view not just of the lighthouse but frequently of whales, too. Local whale-watching cruises depart from Head Harbour Wharf, a couple of miles back down Rt. 174.

McCurdy's Smokehouse, Lubec   Christina Tree

Given the distances covered in this section, we are listing the our lodging choices as they appear geographically, from west to east. The Englishman's Bed and Breakfast (207-546-2337; englishmansbandb.com; 122 Main St.), north of Milbridge in Cherryfield, is a beautifully restored four-square 1793 Federal-style mansion set above the Narragaugus River, with a wide back deck and screened gazebo. Kathy and Peter Winham offer two guest rooms in the house itself and a delightful "guest house" unit with a fridge and hot plate. A full breakfast is served by the 18th-century hearth in the dining room. Cream teas are a specialty.

In Addison, south of Rt. 1, Pleasant Bay Bed & Breakfast (207-483-4490; pleasantbay.com) is a find, a spacious, contemporary house with many windows and a deck overlooking the tidal Pleasant River. Joan Yeaton grew up in the area and returned after raising six children, clearing this land and building the house with her husband, Leon. It's a working llama farm, and guests can meander the wooded trails down to the bay with or without the animals. The four reasonably priced upstairs rooms with water views include one family-sized room with private bath and a lovely two-room suite with a living room, kitchenette, and deck overlooking the water. There are moorings for guests arriving by water.

In Jonesport the best place to stay is Harbor House on Sawyer Cove (207-497-5417; harborhs.com; 27 Sawyer Square). Maureen and Gene Hart have transformed the handsome

Head of Harbour Light, Campobello Island
Joyce Morrell

1880s house into an attractive B&B and antiques store. Two unusually large, attractive upstairs guest rooms overlook the marina and harbor.

Micmac Farm Guesthouses and Gardner House (207-255-3008; micmacfarm.com), off Rt. 92 in Machiasport, is a classic Cape, built by Ebenezer Gardner above the Machias River in 1776; it's also the oldest house in Machias and a real treasure. In summer guests are treated to a large, very private downstairs bedroom furnished in family antiques, with a deck overlooking the river. There are also three comfortable, well-designed housekeeping cabins, each with two double beds and river views.

The core of Riverside Inn (888-255-4344; riversideinn-maine.com) on Rt. 1, East Machias, dates from an 1805 house, but its heart—the first thing guests see—is a professional kitchen. Innkeepers Ellen McLaughlin and Rocky Rakoczy offer fine dining as well as two suites in the Coach House, with decks overlooking the river. There are also two nicely decorated upstairs guest rooms with private bath in the house.

West Quoddy Station (877-535-7414; quoddyvacation.com), the former U.S. Coast Guard station within walking distance of Quoddy Head State Park in South Lubec, has been transformed into six attractive units, nicely furnished with antiques, fitted with phones and TV; upstairs units offer sea views.

In Lubec, Peacock House (207-733-2403; peacockhouse.com; 27 Summer St.), a gracious 1860s house on a quiet side street, was home to four generations of the owners of the major local cannery; the three guest rooms and four suites, one handicapped accessible, are carefully, comfortably furnished. Up the hill Home Port Inn and Restaurant (207-733-2077; home portinn.com; 45 Main St.), another vintage mansion, offers seven tastefully decorated guest rooms and fine dining. Inn at the Wharf (207-733-4400; wharfrentals.com; 69 Johnson St.) was the town's last surviving sardine cannery, recently transformed into spacious suites and two-bedroom,

two-bath apartments, all right on the water. This is also the source of bicycle and kayak rentals.

Across the international bridge, The Owen House (506-752-2977; owenhouse.ca) is reason enough to come to Campobello. Built in 1835 by Admiral William Fitzwilliam Owen, son of the British captain to whom the island was granted in 1769, this is probably the most historic house on the island, and it's a beauty, set on a headland overlooking Passamaquoddy Bay. Joyce Morrell, a watercolor artist who maintains a gallery here, has furnished the nine guest rooms (seven with private bath) with friendly antiques, handmade quilts, and good art. The ferry (see the sidebar) leaves from the neighboring beach.

Local Flavors

The taste of the Bold Coast— local restaurants, cafés, and more

Dining-out options are few and far between along this lonely stretch of coast, so reservations are a must at Riverside Inn (see *Places to Stay*) in East Machias, open for dinner year-round. Specialties include lobster and scallops in champagne butter sauce, and fresh salmon stuffed with shrimp and crabmeat. At the seasonal Home Port Inn (again, detailed in *Places to Stay*) the menu usually includes fresh seafood bouillabaisse and steak au poivre.

New on Lubec's Water St. in 2010: Water Street Tavern (207-733-2477) has great views, atmosphere, and a menu studded with seafood and pasta (lobster mac 'n' cheese is $12). Neigh-

Owen House, Campobello   Christina Tree

boring Frank's Dockside (207-733-4484) is open for lunch as well as dinner with a deck, specializing in the evening in Italian veal and vegetarian classics as well as seafood, from fried clam baskets to crab-stuffed haddock.

As they appear geographically, we have noted 44 Degrees North in Milbridge and Helen's Restaurant in Machias, which is the region's landmark dining spot. Founded in 1950, it's still in the same family, enjoying a new lease on life thanks to current owners David and Julie Barker. Ingredients are as fresh and local as possible. We should also mention Tall Barney's Restaurant (207-497-2403; tallbarneys .com; 52 Main St.) in Jonesport, a legendary gathering spot that was the subject of a National Public Radio story that inspired its present owners to buy it. They are hanging in there but now open just seasonally.

Eastport, Cobscook, and Passamaquoddy Bays

Check out these great attractions and activities . . .

Eastport (eastportchamber.net) is just 3 miles north of Lubec by boat but 43 miles by land around Cobscook Bay. *Cobscook* is said to mean "boiling water" in the Passamaquoddy tongue, and tremendous tides—a tidal range of more than 25 feet—seemingly boil in, sloshing up deep inlets divided by ragged land fingers along the north and south shores.

Cobscook is itself an inlet of larger Passamaquoddy Bay on Eastport's eastern and northern shores. Here the surge of the tide is so powerful that in the 1930s President Roosevelt backed a proposal to harness its energy to electrify much of the northeastern coast. Recently turbines have been submerged off Eastport, a more modest experiment. Old Sow, a whirlpool between Eastport and Deer Island said to be 230 feet in diameter, is reportedly the largest in the Western Hemisphere.

Eastport consists entirely of islands, principally Moose Island, which is connected to Rt. 1 by Rt. 190 via a series of causeways (actually, tidal dams built in the 1930s for the failed tidal power project), linking other islands. It runs through the center of Sipayik, the Pleasant Point Indian Reservation home to some 700 members of the Passamaquoddy Indian tribe. It's home to the Waponahki Museum (207-853-2600; wabanaki .com) and three-day Indian Ceremonial Days in early August.

Music at Peavey Library, Eastport

Christina Tree

Eastport's wealth of Federal and Greek Revival architecture is a reminder that by the War of 1812 this was an important enough port for the British to capture and occupy; their former officers' quarters, now the Barracks Museum (74 Washington St.), houses the town historical collection. Sardine canning in Maine began in Eastport in 1875 and a boom era quickly followed, evoked in the handsome brick commercial buildings along Water St. Welcoming you to town at the point Rt. 190 becomes Washington St., Raye's Mustard Mill (207-853-4451; rayesmustard.com) is another holdover from that era, the country's last remaining stone-ground-mustard mill. The company has been in business since 1900 and today its mustard is Eastport's biggest export, sold throughout the country.

Passamaquoddy sweetgrass baskets at The Shop at the Commons, Eastport

Christina Tree

The current population of this island "city" is less than half what it what was in 1900. Still, it remains a "city" and a working deepwater port, the deepest on the U.S. East Coast. There are many gaps in the old waterfront, now

Donald Southerland and Earth Forms Pottery, Eastport

Christina Tree

riprapped in pink granite to form a seawall. With its flat, haunting light, Eastport has an end-of-the-world feel and suggests an Edward Hopper painting. It's a landscape that draws artists, and there are galleries along Water St. The Commons (thecommonseastport.com; 51 Water St.) displays the works of more than 90 Passamaquoddy Bay artists and artisans, including fabric art, carved burl bowls, pottery, and the best selection of Passamaquoddy sweetgrass baskets. Also check out The Eastport Gallery (207-853-4166; eastportgallery.com; 74 Water St.) and Earth Forms Pottery (207-853-2430; earthforms.biz), Donald Southerland's studio/gallery at the corner of Water and Dana streets. The Tides Institute Museum of Art (207-853-4047; tidesinstitue.org; 43 Water St.) fills an 1880s bank building with a collection of amazing art and archival photographs focusing on Passamaquoddy Bay, as well as changing exhibits. The Eastport Arts Center (207-853-5803; eastportartscenter.com), housed in the vintage-1837 Washington Street Baptist Church, is home to half a dozen arts organizations and a venue for films, concerts, and live performances.

As much as anywhere in Maine, the thing to do here is to get out on the water. Passamaquoddy is a broad, delightful, island-spotted bay. You can explore it on the *Sylvina W. Beal* (207-853-2500; eastportwindjammers.com), an 84-foot schooner that's a veteran of many years of herring and mackerel fishing out of Eastport and Lubec, or via the ferry to Deer Island (see the *Quoddy Loop* sidebar).

Hugh French at the Tides Institute and Museum of Art, Eastport

Christina Tree

Checking In

Best places to stay in Eastport

Kilby House Inn (207-853-0989; kilby houseinn.com; 122 Water St.). This is a Queen Anne–style house on the quiet end of the waterfront with an attractive double parlor that invites you to sit down and read. Innkeeper Gregg Noyes's passions include playing the organ and refinishing antiques. There are five pleasant upstairs guest rooms, including the sunny master with its four-poster canopy bed and water view, and two antiques-furnished rooms with private bath. Reasonable rates includes a very full breakfast. Chadbourne House (888-853-2728; chadbourne house.com; 19 Shackford St.) is a Federal-style mansion with four guest suites, one occupying the entire third floor. Guests are asked to remove their shoes. Upstairs at The Commons (207-

853-4123; thecommonseastport.com) two second-floor, two-bedroom units overlooking the harbor are available by the week. Grandmotherly Ruth McInnis welcome pets at Todd House (207-853-2328), a restored 1775 Cape, while handicapped-accessible Motel East (207-853-4747), overlooking the bay, caters to families with both rates and amenities.

Local Flavors

The taste of Eastport—local restaurants, cafés, and more

The Pickled Herring (207-853-2323; thepickledherring.com; 32 Water St). Eastport native Gary Craig has created a spacious, attractive dining spot with an open kitchen featuring a wood-fired grill, local beers, and produce. Prime rib as well as seafood and pizza (including

The Quoddy Loop

Beyond Eastport you don't drop off the end of the world. On a sunny summer day when the car ferries are running, the crossing on Passamaquoddy Bay to New Brunswick is among the most scenic and satisfying in the East. **East Coast Ferries Ltd.** (877-747-2159; eastcoastferries.nb.ca), based on Deer Island, serves both Campobello Island (30 minutes) and Eastport (20 minutes). The ferries are modified tugs with long, hydraulically operated arms linked to barges. Passengers and bikes, cars, and even buses board on ramps lowered to the beach. Back in deep water the steel arm turns the barge, reversing direction. Service to Deer Isle is frequent and reasonably priced; most passengers continue on across the island and board the larger **New Brunswick Department of Transportation ferries** (506-453-3939). These make the 20-minute run, usually every half hour, to L'Etete, NB, handy to St. Andrews, New Brunswick's Bar Harbor, with great shopping, dining, and more lodging options than all of Washington County combined. Most visitors stay at least a night in St. Andrews and, depending on the weather, drive or ferry back across the bay. This circuit has come to be called the **Quoddy Loop** (quoddyloop.com).

lobster) are the specialties here; reserve a spot by the windows.

Eastport Chowder House (207-853-4700; 167 Water St.), open seasonally for lunch through dinner, is on the bay, said to be the site of the country's first fish and sardine cannery. It's a

Seating at the Quoddy Bay Lobster Co. Eastport   Christina Tree

good bet for lunch, from sandwiches to fish stews and lobster. It's possible to get takeout (and thus park in line) for the ferry that departs from the adjacent beach.

Quoddy Bay Lobster Co. (207-853-6640; 7 Sea St.) is hidden back behind the Tides Institute but well worth finding for its fabulous lobster rolls drizzled with butter, fried clam rolls so thick you have to eat them with a fork, and great fish chowder. Order and eat overlooking the water at picnic tables.

The New Friendly Restaurant (207-853-6610; Rt. 1, Perry), just beyond the turnoff for Eastport, is a homey restaurant with booths and food that's known as the best around: fish stews and chowders, basics like liver and onions, not-so-basics like an elegant crab salad and the most lobster in a lobster sandwich. Beer and wine served.

Raye's Mustard Mill and Pantry (207-853-3351; Rt. 190). Sample the many varieties of mustard in the Pantry, where soup and sandwiches are also served. Tours of the mustard mill are offered year-round, daily on the hour (except the lunch hour).

Index

DATE DUE

NOV 2 3 2011			
FEB 0 9 2012			
FEB 1 7 2015			

GAYLORD   PRINTED IN U.S.A.